THE MOUNT RUSHMORE STORY

THE
M·O·U·N·T
R·U·S·H·M·O·R·E
STORY

by Judith St. George

ILLUSTRATED WITH PHOTOGRAPHS

G. P. PUTNAM'S SONS
New York

Text copyright © 1985 by Judith St. George
All rights reserved.
Published simultaneously in Canada
by General Publishing Co. Limited, Toronto.
Library of Congress Cataloging in Publication Data
St. George, Judith, date.   The Mount Rushmore story.
Bibliography: p.   Includes index.
Summary: A biography of the sculptor who devoted the
last fourteen years of his life to the carving of the
four presidents heads on the face of Mount Rushmore.
1. Borglum, Gutzon, 1867–1941—Juvenile literature.
2. Mount Rushmore National Memorial (S.D.)—Juvenile literature.
[1. Borglum, Gutzon, 1867–1941.   2. Sculptors.
3. Mount Rushmore National Memorial (S.D.)] I. Title.
NB237.B6A68   1985b   730'.92'4   [B]   [92]   84-24963
ISBN 0-399-21117-9
Printed in the United States of America
Book design by Kathleen Westray
First impression

TO MY SON PETER

I would like to thank all those who so generously gave of their time and talent to help me research this book, particularly Tom Haraden, of the National Park Service, Mount Rushmore National Memorial, Keystone, South Dakota, who hiked me up to the top of the heads and provided me with all the assistance any researcher could ask for, as well as reading and commenting on my manuscript.

I would also like to thank Terri Wohlever, Mount Rushmore National Memorial; Donald Frankfort, Geologist, Wind Cave National Park, Hot Springs, South Dakota; Dr. R. T. Theisz, Center of Indian Studies, Black Hills State College, Spearfish, South Dakota; Donna Neal, Devereaux Library, South Dakota School of Mines and Technology, Rapid City, South Dakota; and Mrs. C. Rushmore Patterson, as well as all the former workers who answered my letters of inquiry with fascinating reminiscences of their years at Mount Rushmore.

THE MOUNT RUSHMORE STORY

E V E N by horseback the mountainous route was almost impassable. Certainly there were no roads to follow on that warm August day in 1925. Only an occasional logging trail made the going a little easier. But the guide, state forester Theodore Shoemaker, had lived in the area for forty years and knew these mountains inside out and backwards. For days now, he had been leading his party through the Harney Mountain Range in the Black Hills of South Dakota.

The Black Hills lie like a beating heart near the geographical center of the United States. Only some 120 miles long and 60 miles wide, the Black Hills are a fertile outpost that rise up dramatically from the rolling, treeless Great Plains that surround them. Their steep slopes are thick with dark ponderosa pine forests that from a distance shimmer blue-black. The Sioux Indians called them *Paha Sapa*, the early Spanish explorers *Costa Negra*, and the French voyageurs *Côtes Noires*, all meaning the "hills that are black," or the Black Hills.

But beautiful as the scenery was, Gutzon Borglum headed up the little party that Shoemaker was guiding and Gutzon Borglum wasn't on a sightseeing trip. He was a well-known sculptor and he was on a quest. Dressed in golf knickers, a knitted vest, a flowing ascot tie, and ankle-

Theodore Shoemaker, Gutzon Borglum (seated), and young Lincoln Borglum as they begin their search for the perfect mountain.

high sneakers, Borglum, accompanied by his thirteen-year-old son Lincoln and a local horse wrangler, had inspected one granite peak after another and rejected them all. He knew exactly the kind of mountain he was looking for, and when Gutzon Borglum's mind was set, there was no changing it.

No, that mountain has too many deep cracks. This one faces the wrong direction. Too coarse a grain of granite in that one. Would he ever find it, the perfect mountain on which to carve an enormous sculpture that would symbolize America to the world?

This wasn't Borglum's first trip to the Black Hills. Not only had he stopped in the Hills on his honeymoon sixteen years before, but last year, in September 1924, he and Lincoln had made a quick two-day visit to see if these granite mountains were even a possibility for a sculpture. After climbing Harney Peak, the highest mountain east of the Rockies, Borglum had been so impressed by the beauty of the Hills and the granite mountains, he had called them the "garden of the gods."

"There's the place to carve a great national monument," he announced, promising he would return to find just the right mountain. Now here he and Lincoln were again, a year later, riding through almost impenetrable forest with no success at all.

But on that August day Theodore Shoemaker had a destination in mind, a remote granite mountain northeast of Harney Peak that was unique. He led his party single file through the brush, then waved Borglum on ahead to let him have the first view. There it was. Mount Rushmore. Shoemaker was right. This was it. As Borglum stared up at the ancient seamed rock, he knew he had found his mountain; in one sense his quest was over and in another it was just beginning.

Mount Rushmore rises 6040 feet above sea level, towering 500 feet above any of its neighbors, with a granite face about 1000 feet long and 400 feet high, its east side presenting a 300-foot perpendicular slab. Not only that, but it faces the southeast so that the sun lights up its surface for most of the day. Although the granite had some imperfections, it was finer grained and more evenly textured than any of the other mountains, and the cracks didn't appear to be too deep. It was a moment Gutzon Borglum would never forget as he pulled a notepad from his pocket and began to sketch.

Shoemaker circled his party around Rushmore two or three times, then led them on to view other mountains. But Borglum was impatient. All he could think about was Mount Rushmore, how its craggy face

The ancient face of Mount Rushmore as Borglum first viewed it.

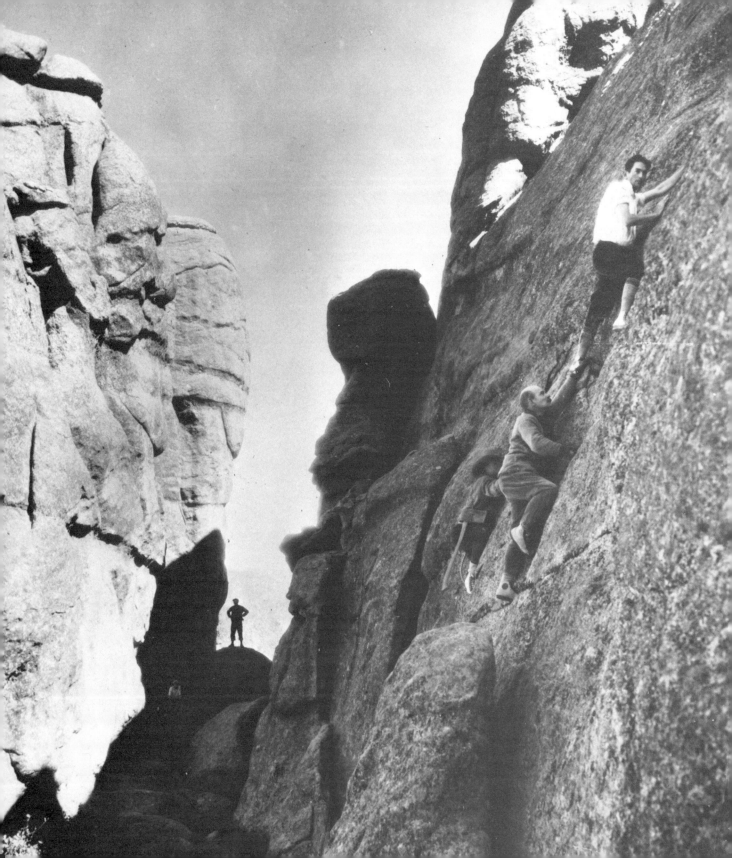

would lend itself to his sculpture, where he would position his figures, and how large they should be. He could hardly wait to get back to it.

But it wasn't until the following week that Borglum and Lincoln, this time with a larger party, returned to Rushmore to camp at its base and climb its steep walls to the top. It was a difficult climb, not just for Borglum who was fifty-eight, but for young Lincoln as well. Attacking the mountain from the canyon behind it, the climbers improvised a kind of ladder out of pine branches crudely nailed together.

"The last 150 feet were almost perpendicular," Lincoln later wrote, "and our climbing methods would hardly be approved by any experienced mountain climber. At one point we pyramided three men on each other's shoulders so the top man could loop his lariat over a projecting sliver of rock!" When they finally reached the summit, they raised the American flag they had brought and took each other's pictures.

Wherever he went, Borglum managed to generate excitement, and the rest of his two-week stay in the Black Hills was no exception. Famous sculptor or no famous sculptor, many South Dakotans raised an outcry when they heard about a possible carving in *their* Black Hills, particularly if it was in the Needles, the sharp, thin granite peaks of the Harney Range that were a source of great local pride. Others objected that a sculpture in those mountains would be so remote no one would be able to get there to see it. And who would finance it?

Although Borglum paid no attention to the uproar, he did reassure everyone that he would not carve in the Needles and make "totem poles of these wonderful spires." And he did pay attention to newspaper reporters. He wanted national publicity to launch this project, and newspapers were the best way to get it. Reporters, who had long ago discovered that Gutzon Borglum could always be counted on for a colorful story, clamored for the interviews, which he was only too happy to give them.

On August 26, 1925, the day Borglum and Lincoln left the Black Hills, Borglum announced in his usual exaggerated style that the carving on Mount Rushmore would be "the greatest thing of its character in the entire world." Only in Gutzon Borglum's mind, the boast wasn't an exaggeration, it was a statement of fact.

Borglum raises the American flag on top of Mount Rushmore.

OPPOSITE: Borglum and his companions climb the back face of Mount Rushmore for the first time, August 1925.

CHAPTER

· 2 ·

T H E R E was no way that Gutzon Borglum could know when he first saw Mount Rushmore in 1925 that its granite face would present a struggle that would last the rest of his life, a struggle with the imperfections of the stone, a struggle for money, a struggle against his critics, a struggle with everyone associated with the project. Even if he had known, he probably would have shrugged it off. Gutzon Borglum had been in the center of controversy as long as anyone could remember, and there was no reason to believe that Mount Rushmore would be any different. "My life has been a one-man war from beginning to date," he stated on his seventy-first birthday.

Much of John Gutzon de la Mothe Borglum's outspoken individualism was shaped by his childhood on the Western frontier. His parents had immigrated to the United States from Denmark in 1864, setting out immediately by wagon train for the Idaho Territory, where Gutzon was born on March 25, 1867, twenty-three years before Idaho became a state.

Borglum wrote of his childhood, "My slates were covered from end to end with portraits of Savonarola, Fra Angelico, and Wild Bill [Hickok] and Sitting Bull; I knew all equally well and admired them about alike; Dante, Angelo [Michelangelo], and Petrarch were my intimate friends, with Crow and Sioux raiding all about. Into this was injected the legends of the Danes, poured into my ears by a Danish mother, while a father talked Socrates till the candle went out."

Intensely patriotic first-generation Americans like the Borglums who were no longer bound by old European class systems believed that by grit, determination, and hard work, they could accomplish anything. And if we can't, they told their children, you can. If one place or job didn't work out, immigrant families would move on, and Gutzon's father and stepmother, along with Gutzon, his brother, and seven half brothers and sisters, moved often, from Idaho to Utah to Missouri to Nebraska, and briefly to California. This optimism for the future and attraction to the frontier life of action were basic to Borglum's constant craving for a challenge, his restlessness, and his lifelong dislike of any kind of restrictions.

During Borglum's first thirty years, which coincided with the last thirty years of the nineteenth century, the nation itself was experiencing a surge of optimism and growth. It was a time when capitalism was the highest form of patriotism, and conservation was an unheard-of philosophy. With the Civil War over, the country, which believed that it was America's manifest destiny to settle the continent from coast to coast, built a new industrial society from steam, electricity, coal, iron, steel, and countless inventions from the light bulb to the automobile.

Only partly in humor, a popular slogan boasted, "The difficult we do at once; the impossible takes a little longer." Single-minded, intense, self-assured, if not cocky, Gutzon Borglum, like the country in which he was raised, never considered that any problem was without a solution or that any project was beyond his ability. He simply stretched his skills to meet the challenge.

Borglum, who had shown an interest in both drawing and western lore since his schoolboy days, decided at the age of seventeen that art would be his life. And it was. After leaving home for California, he struggled to make ends meet for five years, teaching art, painting portraits and western landscapes, and working at odd jobs. In 1889, when he was twenty-two, Borglum married Lisa Putnam, a widow of forty. The following year, the two of them set off for Europe, where Borglum studied his craft under a new friend, the famous French sculptor Auguste Rodin. As the years passed, Borglum, who was now turning more and more to sculpture himself, became well known, receiving commissions in both the United States and Europe.

But as Borglum's career flourished, his marriage floundered, and in 1908 he and Lisa were divorced. The following year, he married Mary Montgomery, who gave up her own promising career when she married "Dane," as she called him. James Lincoln was born to the Borglums in 1912, and Mary Ellis in 1916. By the time of his second marriage, Borglum had given up painting almost entirely and was concentrating on naturalistic sculpture, usually on a grand scale.

Borglum's work, which expressed both vitality and emotion, included figures for the Cathedral of St. John the Divine in New York City, the large head of Lincoln in the rotunda of the national Capitol building, a bronze statue of General Philip H. Sheridan, and a bronze seated Lincoln. Although art critics of the time rated Borglum as good but not outstanding, the American public understood and liked his brand of energetic naturalism, and he acquired a solid reputation.

In 1915 the Stone Mountain Confederate Monumental Association commissioned Borglum to carve a memorial on Stone Mountain near Atlanta, Georgia, to commemorate the Confederate army in the Civil War. With his usual enthusiasm, Borglum planned an enormous sculpture that would march Confederate leaders, cavalry, artillery, and foot soldiers across a quarter mile of mountain face.

But shortly after Borglum's head of Robert E. Lee was unveiled in 1924, a serious disagreement arose between the opinionated Borglum and the equally opinionated president of the Stone Mountain Association about which one of them was in charge of the sculpture. Borglum, who had an almost compulsive need to control every phase of a project, had never worked well with committees, and he didn't work well with this one. The question about who was in charge was decisively answered in 1925 when the Association fired Borglum. Never one to take such a decision lightly, Borglum promptly destroyed his studio models of the sculpture so that no other artist could use them to continue *his* work on the mountain. Although the furious Stone Mountain Association issued a warrant for his arrest, Borglum had already fled the state.

It was at this low moment in Borglum's career that he was presented with the opportunity to carve a mountain sculpture in the Black Hills. The idea was the brainchild of Doane Robinson, secretary and historian of the South Dakota Historical Society, who in 1923, at the age of sixty-six, dreamed up the project as a tourist attraction for the state. After traveling all over South Dakota trying without success to stir up interest, Robinson finally sat down and wrote Borglum asking him if he would

Borglum in his studio, working on a model of his Gettysburg memorial statue.

"design and supervise a massive sculpture" in the Black Hills. Borglum's reaction? A resounding yes!

Almost fanatically patriotic, Borglum, who believed that the nation's westward expansion, as well as its growth as a democracy, was unmatched in world history, leaped at the chance to immortalize America. The fact that in the doing he would be immortalized as well could hardly have escaped his notice. As to the size of the sculpture, the bigger the better. For years Borglum had been advocating art on a colossal scale. "My big mission in life is to get the American people to look at art in a big way and to get away from this petty stuff," he once commented.

Doane Robinson's letter arrived at a perfect time. Now Borglum could put the Stone Mountain unpleasantness behind him and begin a new and even more challenging project. Having Borglum on board suited Robinson too. He needed action and publicity for his proposed sculpture and with Borglum, he was assured of both. There was no question that Borglum was his own best press agent. When Robinson asked him to set a date to visit the Black Hills, Borglum wired back, "About September 25, on condition there shall be no publicity not released by me."

Borglum had never been content to be solely an artist, and with his flamboyant personality as well as his passion for the limelight, he inevitably made news. Over the years, he had been interested in—and had expressed controversial opinions about—writing, aircraft design, politics, international affairs, prizefighting, and especially American art and American taste in art. Complaining about his countrymen's fondness for the artistic past, he commented, "We won't look at anything unless it wears a helmet or Greek sandals." Now he was about to tackle something both big *and* American.

As soon as Gutzon Borglum and Lincoln left the Black Hills in August 1925 after their second visit, Doane Robinson got down to the serious business of trying to raise money. By now he had enlisted the interest of Peter Norbeck, the popular United States senator from South Dakota who had designed many miles of scenic roads throughout the Black Hills, and who had been the driving force behind the creation of the Hills' Custer State Park in 1919, at that time the largest state park in the country. But even with Norbeck's help, Robinson faced a lot of opposition as he traveled around the state.

Unfortunately, the still bitter members of the Stone Mountain Association had flooded South Dakota with letters and pamphlets giving their side of the controversy as well as attacking Borglum personally. Although

Peter Norbeck's scenic roads wind through the Needles.

both parties had been at fault, the Stone Mountain Association perhaps even more than Borglum, many South Dakotans took the propaganda seriously and were dead set against having Borglum head up a similar project in their state.

At a time when there were no organized environmental groups and conservation was only a whisper, newspaper editorials were often the only voice raised, and South Dakota newspapers almost unanimously opposed the sculpture project. The Rapid City, South Dakota, *Daily Journal* stated that the Black Hills could sell themselves without any "alteration on nature's handiwork." The Yankton, South Dakota, newspaper wrote, "We who live out on the plains are quite satisfied with the beauties of our great Black Hills as bequeathed to us by nature." One paper summed up the whole idea as "bunk!" An Eastern newspaper joined in. "Borglum is about to destroy another mountain. Thank God it is in South Dakota where no one will ever see it."

Although all sorts of objections were raised, surprisingly enough, if any reference was made at the time to Sioux Indian rights in the affair, that reference is now lost. More than any other interest group, the Sioux had a long-time stake in Paha Sapa, the hills that are black, taken from them illegally less than fifty years before.

W H A T an irony that Mount Rushmore was within the boundaries of both Harney National Forest and Custer State Park, among two of the most hated names in the Sioux tradition. In 1854 General William S. Harney with a force of 1200 men attacked a Sioux village, massacring eighty-six Sioux, including women and children. General George Armstrong Custer, who was one of the most famous "Indian fighters" in the United States Army, had, like Harney, attacked a sleeping Indian village, killing 103 Indians, only eleven of whom were warriors, as well as taking fifty-three women and children captive and slaughtering hundreds of Indian ponies. Both men had led expeditions into the Black Hills, Harney in 1855 and Custer in 1874, in direct violation of treaties the United States government had signed with the Sioux.

Although the word *Sioux* is actually a French abbreviation of the Chippewa word *Nadewisou,* it is the name the people of the Dakota Nation have come to be called, and even come to call themselves. In the 1600s, the three Sioux tribes, the Santees, the Yanktons, and the Tetons, were woodland Indians living near the western Great Lakes. Gradually, they moved west, the Santee Sioux settling permanently in Minnesota, with the Yankton Sioux migrating to the prairie country of eastern North and South Dakota. It was the Teton Sioux tribe, larger than the Santee and Yankton tribes combined, that made its home bordering on the Black Hills, and to whom the term *Sioux* hereafter refers.

The "golden years" of the Sioux were between 1800 and 1840–50. With the acquisition of horses, and the adoption of a nomadic life-style, they evolved from wandering, isolated bands into the most powerful Indian tribe on the North American continent. Although the Cheyenne and Crow dominated the country north and west of the Black Hills, the Sioux controlled all of the Great Plains west of the Missouri River, including the Black Hills and parts of eastern Wyoming. Because the Sioux had no written records other than their pictorial calendars, much of their history has been lost; what hasn't been lost was how they felt, and still feel, about the Black Hills, their sacred Paha Sapa.

To them, Paha Sapa was the place of spirits and holy mountains where sacred ceremonies were held and where the Thunder Powers caused thunder and shooting fire (lightning) to dance and jump from peak to peak. Paha Sapa was reserved for the spirits of dead warriors, to accustom their eyes to beauty so that they wouldn't be blinded by their first view of Paradise. More important, it was where young warriors came alone for their vision quests to allow Wakan Tanka, the Great Spirit, to guide the course of their future lives.

Because it was a holy place, no Sioux lived in Paha Sapa, although from time to time they ventured in to cut down pine trees to use for their tipi poles, or to collect rocks for making tools and weapons, or to harvest plants for their dyes and medicines. Occasionally, when buffalo were scarce, the Sioux would enter Paha Sapa to hunt for deer or elk or other game. But basically Paha Sapa was revered and feared as the heart of Sioux land and the center of their spiritual life.

Just as the tribe respected each brave's personal vision and the direction in which that vision led him, so too did Sioux society respect each individual and that individual's opinion. In this democracy, the young and strong took care of the old and weak, and all game from the hunt was shared. There were no written laws as we know them, and no permanent leaders, although every man, woman, and child was aware of his or her role in the life of the tribe, the most important attribute being to act as a good and responsible relative. To do wrong was to invite the disapproval or ridicule of the tribe, even banishment, the worst punishment of all.

With Paha Sapa at the center of Sioux spiritual life, the bison, or buffalo, as North America's largest land animal is known, was at the center of their culture and economy. The survival of the tribe depended on the buffalo, its wanderings, its habits, its abundance or scarcity. Buffalo hair, hide, hoof, bones, skull, entrails, tail, chips (dried dung), not to mention meat, were used for clothing, shelter, tools, weapons, fuel, and food. One anthropologist has documented eighty-seven ways the Plains Indians used the buffalo, or *Tatanka*.

As to the land, it came from the Great Spirit and could no more be owned than the sky. Unfortunately, the United States government and its people viewed land differently, and during those years of the nineteenth century when the Sioux were at the peak of their power, America was beginning to eye their land jealously. Land was what America needed, land for the thousands of immigrants like the Borglums who were flooding the country from Europe, land that was rich in gold and precious minerals, land teeming with valuable fur-bearing animals, land on which to build railroads, land to fence in for domestic livestock.

But the Plains Indians, the Cheyennes, the Arapahoes, and especially the Sioux, who controlled the Dakota Territory from the Missouri River west into the Powder River Country and south into Nebraska, including the Black Hills, were not about to turn over their traditional buffalo hunting grounds to anyone. Nevertheless, the trickle of wagon trains that passed through their land on the way to California and Oregon and the goldfields of Montana soon became a flood. As more and more wagon trains rumbled by, and as the railroads extended their reach westward, the Sioux realized that their way of life was being seriously threatened. When Sioux raids on wagon trains became more aggressive, the United States government ordered the army to build and maintain forts along the wagon trails.

The Sioux Wars that followed the arrival of the United States Army extended from 1854 to 1890, with encounters that resulted in death and lasting bitterness on both sides. It is interesting to note that during those terrible years Sioux victories over professional armed soldiers were called massacres, while Army victories over the Sioux, which often included the slaughter of whole villages, were called battles.

Although concerned peace groups in the East lobbied for Indian rights, they had little effect on the government's belligerent policy of viewing the Indians as an enemy foreign nation. General William T. Sherman, Commander of the West from 1865 to 1869, summed up this attitude when he said, "We must act with vindictive earnestness against the Sioux, even to their extermination, men, women, and children."

General Philip H. Sheridan, who succeeded Sherman as Commander of the West from 1869 to 1883, was equally outspoken. "The only good Indians I ever saw were dead," was his oft-quoted comment, Sheridan himself being the subject of two large and flattering equestrian statues by Gutzon Borglum.

Warfare was one way of dealing with the Sioux, while treaties were another. Unfortunately, the government honored a treaty only until it wanted to acquire more Indian land, while the Sioux believed that because the Great Spirit owned the land, there was no way it could be sold. "One does not sell the earth upon which the people walk," declared the Sioux warrior Crazy Horse. Besides, in the democracy that was Sioux society, no man could speak, let alone "touch the pen" in a treaty for the whole tribe, despite what United States government officials believed.

No matter how the Sioux viewed the treaties, and certainly they, as well as the government, broke treaties often, those signed pieces of paper

Prisoners captured by General Custer during the Sioux Campaign, 1868.

made it possible for the United States to justify legally the takeover of the Sioux land it wanted so badly. In 1868, the famous Fort Laramie Treaty created for the exclusive use of the Sioux the 41,000-square-mile Great Sioux Reservation which included all of South Dakota west of the Missouri River as well as the Black Hills, while the Powder River Country between the Black Hills and the Bighorn Mountains was to be "unceded Indian territory." The treaty, which was signed by both General Harney and General Sherman, among others, promised that the Great Sioux Reservation would be "set apart for the absolute and undisturbed use and occupation of the Indians . . . and the United States now solemnly agrees that no persons . . . shall ever be permitted to pass over, settle upon, or reside in the territory . . ."

Because sufficient numbers of buffalo still roamed that part of the country, for a few years there were only occasional skirmishes between the Sioux and the Army. But rumors of gold in the Black Hills had circu-

Indian leaders meet with General Harney (white beard), General Sherman, and other peace commissioners to sign the Fort Laramie Treaty, 1868.

lated for a long time, and in 1874 General Custer was ordered into the Black Hills at the head of over a thousand men, supposedly to survey for a possible fort site, although his well-publicized expedition included two miners and a geologist. In direct violation of the Fort Laramie Treaty, Custer and his forces followed what the Sioux called "The Thieves' Road" for three weeks in the Hills, where early in August, his miners found what the nation had been hoping for. GOLD! THE LAND OF PROMISE-STIRRING NEWS FROM THE BLACK HILLS headlined a Chicago newspaper on August 27, 1874.

Because the United States Senate had pledged its word of honor when it ratified the Fort Laramie Treaty, the government made a halfhearted attempt to keep its gold-hungry citizens out of the Black Hills. But the country was in the middle of an economic depression, the Panic of 1873, and with twenty percent of all non-farm workers out of work, there was no stopping the gold rush even if the government had really wanted to. By the end of 1875, the Black Hills were overrun by prospectors, and by 1876 an estimated 10,000 people had poured into the area.

The solution, the government decided, was to buy the Black Hills, an impossibility when the Sioux tribal leaders shrewdly put a $70,000,000 price tag on the land. The government, in turn, offered $400,000 a year for the mineral rights, or $6,000,000 in fifteen annual installments, an offer which was promptly rejected by the Sioux, both the "friendlies" and the "hostiles."

The Sioux refusal forced the government to seek another solution. In December 1875 President Grant ordered all Indians in the unceded territory of Wyoming and Montana to move onto government agencies, or reservations, by January 31, 1876. It was, of course, impossible even to convey the order to the widespread Sioux in the dead of winter, let alone for them to obey, and when the government deadline had come and gone, no Sioux had appeared. That, announced the Army, was a declaration of war.

And war it was, all-out war, with the largest Army force ever mustered on the Plains, and the largest Sioux force ever mustered as well. Despite stunning Sioux victories in 1876 at the Rosebud, and particularly at Little Big Horn, where Sitting Bull and Crazy Horse completely annihilated General Custer and his elite 7th Cavalry, in the long run, the Sioux were no match for the United States Army. By 1877, Crazy Horse was a prisoner and Sitting Bull and his small band had retreated temporarily into Canada.

Those Indians who had surrendered were now herded onto reserva-

General Custer's camp at French Creek in the Black Hills where gold was discovered, August 1874.

tions where they were deprived of their hunting tools, horses, and weapons, leaving them totally dependent on government rations. When the government threatened to withhold those rations, the starving Sioux were forced to enter into an agreement by which they turned over the Powder River Country and the Black Hills to the government, more than seven million acres. With no money changing hands, the government promised to provide the Sioux with subsistence rations for as long as necessary for survival in exchange for the land. Many years later the United States Court of Claims said about the affair, "A more ripe and rank case of dishonorable dealings will never, in all probability, be found in our history . . ."

Now *all* the Sioux were moved onto the Great Sioux Reservation, now greatly reduced in size. Most of them were assigned to the Pine Ridge Agency, some thirty miles from the Black Hills, although many of them were moved east of the Missouri River, which their ancestors had crossed four generations earlier. In 1889 the Great Sioux Reservation was further broken up into five separate reservations.

Although the Sioux warriors had been described by General George A. Crook as the "finest natural cavalry that ever existed," being superb horsemen had not been enough. The individualism on which the Sioux prided themselves worked against them in battle. Although capable of incredible bravery, no man took or gave orders, and no one leader assumed command, held the war party together as a unit, mapped out strategy, or enforced discipline. Nor did famous warriors like Sitting Bull and Crazy Horse pursue and attack the enemy after a victory. Only on a few occasions did they go beyond the traditional strike-and-run techniques they were accustomed to using in their limited tribal wars.

Other calamities had already weakened their forces. The white man's railroad transported troops, while the telegraph kept the divisions of the army in touch with their command. Over the years the white man's smallpox, tuberculosis, measles, and cholera had killed thousands of Indians. And then there was the white man's alcohol, to which the Indian was unaccustomed.

But in the long run, it was the death of the buffalo that defeated the Sioux. The Oregon Trail, the Bozeman Trail, and the railroads all disrupted traditional buffalo feeding grounds, while the emigrants' livestock trampled and overgrazed the Plains grasses. But it was the white man's wanton killing that brought the buffalo to the edge of extinction and destroyed the Plains Indians' way of life forever.

"The Buffalo Hunters have done more in the last two years to settle the vexed Indian Question, than the entire regular army in the last thirty years" was General Sheridan's observation. Thousands of buffalo were shot for sport from moving trains, their carcasses left to rot. White hunters slaughtered the buffalo for their skins, sometimes only for their tongues, which were sold as a delicacy for twenty-five cents apiece. The numbers tell it all. In 1850, there were anywhere from thirty to sixty million buffalo. By 1889, there were 550.

Shooting buffalo for sport on the Great Plains from a train.

In 1890, in their mutual distress, Indians on reservations all across the country adopted a new, nonviolent religion known as the Ghost Dance. If the dance was performed faithfully, the earth would soon be covered with new soil, fresh grass, and trees that would bury all the white men. The dead Indian warriors would return, the great herds of buffalo and wild horses would once again roam the earth, and no Indian wearing a holy ghost shirt could be harmed by white bullets. Frightened by the intensity and zeal with which Indians, particularly the Sioux, danced themselves into exhaustion, white authorities demanded protection and the army was called in.

After Sitting Bull was assassinated on Standing Rock Reservation in 1890 as a suspected leader of the Ghost Dance, many of his followers joined Chief Big Foot, a Sioux leader of the Dance who had fled the nearby Cheyenne River Agency in the bitter cold with a band of 120 men and 230 women and children. Hunted down by Custer's old 7th Cavalry, Big Foot's band was overtaken and escorted back to a camp on Wounded Knee Creek. While the soldiers were disarming the Indians, a rifle discharged, alarming both sides and immediately setting off hand-to-hand combat between the soldiers and the mostly unarmed Sioux.

In the confusion that resulted, soldiers opened fire with four Hotchkiss machine guns, with which they had surrounded the camp, instantly killing men, women, and children with the big guns that fired almost a shell a second. Those who survived fled in panic, but the soldiers pursued them through the snow, some for as far as two miles, and cut them down. The known Sioux dead, numbering 153, with some estimates going as high as three hundred, were buried unceremoniously in a mass grave. The twenty-five soldiers who died and the thirty who were wounded were for the most part strafed by their own bullets and shrapnel.

The next day enraged Sioux warriors waged a hopeless battle against the cavalry a few miles from Pine Ridge Agency headquarters. With the Massacre of Wounded Knee on December 29, 1890, and the following day's encounter, the Sioux Wars ended forever, and this time, there was no doubt in anyone's mind as to which side had been massacred.

An unidentified old Sioux warrior later summed up the tragedy of his people. "They made us many promises, more than I can remember, but they never kept but one; they promised to take our land and they took it."

AT least Mount Rushmore wasn't named for an Indian fighter or an army general. Even more improbably, it was named for a New York City lawyer, Charles E. Rushmore, who made several trips on legal business to the Black Hills in 1884 and 1885. Forty years later, in 1925, he wrote to Doane Robinson describing how the mountain had been named for him.

"Late in 1883 the discovery of tin in the Black Hills was brought to the attention of a group of gentlemen in New York City and excited their interest. I was a youthful attorney at the time, and was employed by these gentlemen early in 1884 to go to the Black Hills and secure options on the Etta Mine and other casserite locations. My mission required me to remain several weeks in the Hills, and to return there on two or three later occasions in that year and in 1885. Part of my time was spent among prospectors at Harney, and at a log cabin camp built in that neighborhood. In my life among these rough, but kindly, men I conformed to their ways, and, may I say it with becoming modesty, was in favor with them.

"I was deeply impressed with the Hills, and particularly with a mountain of granite rock that rose above the neighboring peaks. On one occasion while looking from near its base, with almost awe, at this majestic pile, I asked of the men who were with me for its name. They said it had no name, but one of them then spoke up and said 'We will name it now, and name it Rushmore Peak.' That was the origin of the name it bears, and, as I have been informed, it is called Rushmore Peak, Rushmore Mountain and also Rushmore Rock."

And so a Black Hills prospector haphazardly named what would become one of the most famous mountains in the world after a visiting New York lawyer. Over the years, attempts have been made to change the name, but in 1930 the United States Board of Geographic Names settled the issue once and for all by officially recognizing "Mount Rushmore."

Because the Harney Mountain Range, which was to be the site of the carving, was located partially in a national forest and partially in a state park, it was decided that both federal and state laws should be passed to allow work to begin. That way, all bases would be covered in case Borglum changed his mind and decided on a mountain other than Rushmore. Congress quickly passed a law in 1925 to permit the carving on one of the oldest mountain ranges in the world, an act that would be considerably more difficult, if not impossible, in today's environmentally conscious climate. Although the South Dakota state legislature also passed a law, it took a good deal longer to do so, its reluctance prompted not by environmental reasons, but by concern over who would pay for the project.

During the time these two laws were being considered, Borglum was considering an important issue himself. Whose heads would he carve in the granite of Mount Rushmore? When Doane Robinson first suggested the idea of a mountain carving, he had had western heroes in mind— Lewis and Clark, James Bridger, Chief Red Cloud, John Frémont. But Borglum rejected those possibilities outright, his vision being much grander. He felt that these men were too local for a sculpture that would last half a million years or so. "Art in America should be drawn from American sources, memorializing American achievement," he had said earlier, and this was his opportunity to create a monument that would convey the meaning of America to the world.

Despite his years of art study in Paris, London, and Spain, Borglum was first and foremost a patriot whose early paintings and sculptures of western landscapes, horses, Indians, stage coaches, and cowboys expressed his passion for the dramatic story of America's westward expansion. And because the America of the 1920s respected bigness above all, Borglum wanted to make certain that size was an essential part of his carving too. Borglum, who had always been attracted to the colossal art of history, the Great Sphinx of Egypt, the Greek Colossus of Rhodes, the 110-foot Roman statue of Nero, often said, "A monument's dimensions should be determined by the importance to civilization of the events commemorated." And there was no doubt in his mind that this monument should be very large indeed.

By mid 1925 Borglum, who never claimed to be carving the four greatest men in American history, had chosen four presidents for his sculpture: George Washington, Thomas Jefferson, Abraham Lincoln, and Theodore Roosevelt, as symbols of the founding, growth, preservation, and development of the nation. To Borglum, these four men embodied what he believed to be the cornerstone of this country. "Man has a right to be free and to be happy," he said. "These eleven words are the heart and soul of western civilization. These eleven words are the motive back of the Mount Rushmore National Memorial . . . commemorating America's political accomplishment."

There was never any question about George Washington. To Borglum, he represented America's independence, Constitution, liberty, and with that in mind, he positioned Washington as the dominant figure on the mountain, somewhat detached from the others and projecting out the farthest, like the prow of a ship navigating in unknown seas. Furthermore, as a young man, Washington had extensively surveyed what was then the western wilderness, the Virginia Piedmont, the Shenandoah Valley, and the Allegheny region. Washington's travels were in keeping with Borglum's own interest in westward expansion. Borglum modeled the Washington head after portraits by Gilbert Stuart and Rembrandt Peale, as well as the life mask that the French sculptor Jean Antoine Houdon had made of Washington while visiting Mount Vernon in 1785. The life mask, a popular art form of Washington's time, is made by applying a soft material such as plaster or wax to the subject's face. After the material hardens and is removed, it serves as a mold from which a life mask can be cast in plaster, wax, or any other suitable material.

Thomas Jefferson, who had drafted the Declaration of Independence, was president in 1803 when the United States bought the Louisiana Territory from France, doubling the nation's land mass at a cost of about three cents an acre, one of the great real estate bargains of all time. And it was President Jefferson, with his intense concern in westward expansion,

Portrait of George Washington by Gilbert Stuart.

Thomas Jefferson, a detail from John Trumbull's *Signing of the Declaration of Independence.*

who sent Lewis and Clark on their famous expedition to explore a land route to the Pacific Ocean, a journey that eventually opened the West to settlement. Despite his interest in the country's western development, Borglum, using the life mask of Jefferson by American sculptor John H. I. Browere as a guide, modeled Jefferson as he looked at thirty-three, his age when he wrote the Declaration of Independence; this is the only figure of the four sculpted prior to his presidency. It was a decision that turned out to be somewhat of a problem, as the public wasn't familiar with Jefferson's image at that age, and during the carving years, occasionally mistook Jefferson for Martha Washington!

Borglum, who once said of himself, "I was born in the Golden West . . . ," admired Abraham Lincoln more than any other American and named his only son after him. When Lincoln was born in 1809, his backwoods Kentucky birthplace was on the edge of the western frontier. A rude log cabin, the death of his young mother, forests inhabited by wild animals, and less than a full year of schooling were all part of Lincoln's western boyhood. Born in a log cabin himself as well as also losing his mother at an early age, Borglum described Lincoln as "that simple great first gift of the west."

Abraham Lincoln was Borglum's favorite sculpture subject. Borglum first measured and studied Clark Mills's life mask of Lincoln from every angle, and then worked from six photographs of Lincoln which he considered to be particularly accurate. He considered sculpting Lincoln clean-shaven, but decided that on such a huge face, the beard Lincoln wore during his presidency would add strength and contrast to the composition as a whole. Somehow, Borglum's deep compassion for Lincoln as a man and his respect for Lincoln's ability to hold the country together through the crisis of the Civil War shone through his work, and critics consider the Lincoln head to be the best of the four.

In his youth, Theodore Roosevelt had forged strong ties to the Dakota Territory. In 1884, when both his twenty-three-year-old wife and his mother died on the same day, a grief-stricken Roosevelt had retreated to the two cattle ranches he owned in the Dakota Territory to take on the hard life of a working cowboy. When he returned to New York two years later, he was physically and emotionally renewed, prepared to pick up the pieces of his private and political life. It was as if his time in the Dakota Territory had been his own personal vision quest that had guided his future in the direction it should take. "I am, myself, at heart as much a Westerner as an Easterner," he once told a South Dakota audience.

Borglum, who had been born only nine years after Roosevelt, had known and admired Roosevelt personally, and in many ways, the two men were alike, energetic, outspoken, egotistical, headline seekers, with an ability to think and act on a grand scale. They were similar physically too, short and stocky, with strong expressive faces and bristling mustaches, although Borglum, unlike Roosevelt, had been bald from an early age.

The public was ready to accept Washington, Jefferson, and Lincoln, but Borglum's choice of Theodore Roosevelt for the fourth head raised an immediate protest. Roosevelt had only been dead for six years, and time hadn't yet given perspective to his presidency. President Calvin Coolidge, Senator Norbeck, and others strongly favored Roosevelt because he had curbed the power of big business. Borglum, his mind set on the "Nation Builders," saw in Roosevelt's building of the Panama Canal the link that joined the Atlantic and Pacific and fulfilled Columbus's dream of finding a water route to the Far East. Whatever their various reasons, Borglum and the planners of the sculpture united on their decision to include Roosevelt, regardless of public opinion. Borglum modeled the head after a bust of Roosevelt he had sculpted in 1918, a year before Roosevelt's death.

Borglum, determined to have Roosevelt's face on Mount Rushmore, was also determined to have a huge entablature, or panel, in the shape of the Louisiana Purchase, next to the four heads. Carved in eight-foot-high, five-inch-deep gilded letters would be the nine great events in American history, or at least those nine events that Borglum considered to be great: the signing of the Declaration of Independence, the framing of the Constitution, the purchase of the Louisiana Territory, the admission of Texas to the Union, and the acquisition of five territories—Florida, California, Oregon, Alaska, and the Panama Canal Zone.

From the time the memorial was first suggested, all sorts of additional heads have been suggested. If Theodore Roosevelt goes up, argued the Democrats, then we have to have Woodrow Wilson. Franklin D. Roosevelt, Dwight D. Eisenhower, and John F. Kennedy have all been mentioned over the years, as well as Susan B. Anthony, whose inclusion was strongly backed in the 1930s by Eleanor Roosevelt and various women's groups.

But having to decide on a fifth head didn't concern Borglum. He knew he would have a hard enough time fitting in four. From beginning to end, it was the quality of the granite that determined where the heads

Abraham Lincoln, photographed by Mathew Brady, 1862.

Theodore Roosevelt in the 1880s as a working cowboy.

work, Borglum molded a plaster
... he planned to copy on a larger
s... the drilling and blasting re-
m... hidden cracks and flaws were
di... at he wasn't going to be able
to... was forced to cut the plaster
mo... into nine different arrange-
me... y deciding on their perma-
nen...

to t... to sculpt the figures down
to th... rock coat turned out to be
shal... ereby forcing Borglum to
shor... difficult to carve because
of hu... e found near the end of
Linco... anite was discovered on
Roose... ed by four deep fissures,
or cra... ugh the mountain at a
forty-f... ft to right. On the plus
side, L... back, but because the
quality... able to move Lincoln
forward... e time and expense of
taking o...

In o... rock and avoid flaws,
Borglum... equently, dropping or
tilting th... o the right or left. In
the end, i... re itself that dictated
how and ...

Borglum working on an early ver-
sion of his studio model, with Jefferson on Washington's right and
Roosevelt not yet included.

CHAPTER
· 5 ·

T H E Black Hills, which are mountains and not really hills at all, are one of the oldest geological formations on earth, older than the Andes Range and the Alps. At a time when the Black Hills had already formed, the Himalayas were still not much more than a great brackish marsh.

Once, according to Sioux legend, the land was flat and there were no Black Hills at all. It was during a time in history when a decision had to be made, would man eat buffalo, or would buffalo eat man? Only a race could settle the question, so all the animals and birds of the world, including the giant insects and huge animals that once roamed the earth but are no longer seen, came together in Paha Sapa.

They crowded the racetrack, the larger animals trampling the smaller ones, and the birds overhead screeching and squawking. At a signal, they all took off, running and flying as fast as they could, with the huge crush of beasts circling the track like a snake pursuing its own tail.

Before the runners could finish the race, a huge blister began to bulge out of the earth right in the center of the racetrack. The ground shuddered and trembled as the blister erupted with a deafening explosion. Flames shot skyward, covering the runners with lava and smoke, killing them all. When the air cleared, jagged mountains towered up high above the smoldering racetrack, and although no one ever knew who won the race, the magpie had been leading the birds, and Unkche Ghila, a dinosaur which no living person has ever seen, had been ahead of the other animals.

And that, concludes the legend, is how the Great Spirit created the Black Hills. Certainly the legend must be true, because even today, a barren valley of sandy red soil that looks like a racetrack runs almost completely around the Black Hills, and huge dinosaur bones are still found in the racetrack's red earth.

In a simplified way, this Sioux legend helps explain how the Black Hills were formed geologically. All the earth is covered by a hard outside crust three to thirty miles thick that is composed of three kinds of rock: igneous, sedimentary, and metamorphic. Except on steep mountains and in regions of ice and snow, the top of the crust is covered by soil, a thin layer of material created by the weathering of rock and the decay of plant and animal remains.

Igneous rock derives its name from the Latin word meaning "fire," an appropriate name. Igneous rock is formed by the cooling of magma, hot melted mineral material that flows deep within the earth. Sometimes the hot magma pushes right up through the earth's crust in the form of lava erupting from a volcano, while at other times, the magma pushes up a solid dome like a huge blister without breaking through the earth's crust at all.

Sedimentary rock is rock that has "settled." Flowing brooks and rivers carry sediment with them, sediment being clay, silt, sand, pebbles, gravel, and in flood stages, even cobbles and boulders. As brooks and rivers approach a lake or sea, they slow down and drop their load of sediment, which settles to the bottom of that lake or sea, sometimes burying plants and the shells of sea animals. Tremendous deposits are built up as layers of these sediments settle on top of one another. The weight of the upper layers squeezes out all the moisture from the lower layers and gradually presses them solid into what is known as sedimentary rock.

The third family of rocks, metamorphic rock, results when under certain circumstances, internal forces such as earth movements, pressure, heat, and water change sedimentary rock and, less frequently, igneous rock into completely different rock forms. For instance, internal forces can change the sedimentary rock limestone into marble, or the igneous rock granite into gneiss. Any rock whose original form has been permanently changed is called metamorphic rock, the word *metamorphic* coming from the Greek word meaning "change shape."

About two and a half billion years ago, or perhaps even earlier, that section of America where the Black Hills lie was covered by a shallow inland sea, with gravel, sand, clay, and pebbles settling to its bottom. Over the following millions of years, these various materials, as well as microscopic forms of life which lived on the sea floor, packed down and hardened into sedimentary rock. Over a long period of time, heat and pressure converted this sedimentary rock into the metamorphic rock, mica schist. Other forces also played their part. Almost one and a half billion years ago, hot liquid magma from below squeezed into the older mica schist before cooling and crystallizing into the igneous rock granite.

Geologists can only speculate what went on for the next one billion years, their best guess being that it was a long period of erosion. What geologists know for certain, however, is that at the end of that period, beginning about five hundred million years ago, a series of seas advanced and retreated over the Black Hills area, all of them piling sediment on top of the rocks already formed. The floor of these shallow seas was layered with all three rock forms, metamorphic mica schist being the oldest, igneous granite next, and the newest rock, sedimentary rock, on the top. Finally, about sixty million years ago, pressures from below slowly, very slowly, began to push these layers up into an elongated dome about 120 miles long and sixty miles wide that resembled a sheaf of wet newspapers bunching up in the middle as it is pushed from the edges. The Black Hills were born.

With the Sioux racetrack legend in mind, the relatively young sedimentary rock of sandstone and limestone that was deposited last in the sea appears on the outer edges of the Hills, forming the treeless valley that looks like a racetrack, as well as the racetrack's walls. The racetrack itself, which is anywhere from a narrow band to several miles wide, is composed of sandstone, sandy clay, and shales, all sedimentary rocks that have weathered over the years into a sandy red soil.

The racetrack's outer wall, a hard sandstone ridge called the Dakota Sandstone hogback, rises abruptly from the surrounding Plains. The inner wall of the racetrack is a limestone plateau of sedimentary rock known as Pahasapa Limestone. The many miles of caves found in this inner wall were produced by acid groundwater seeping into the crevices and cracks of the porous limestone. As the water gradually dissolved the limestone,

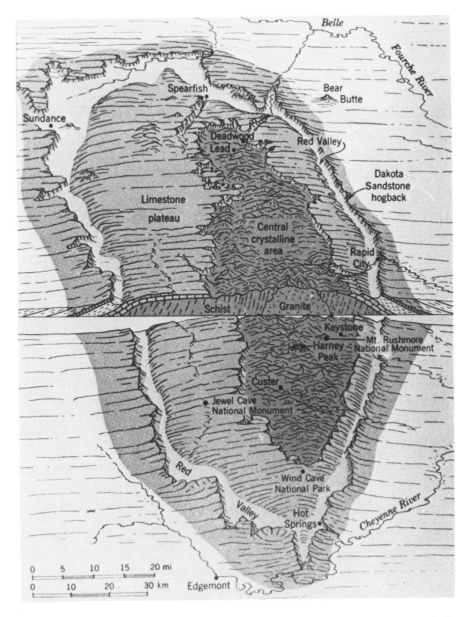

Diagram of the Black Hills.

underground caverns and passages were opened, creating some of the most extensive cave systems in the world.

And it is here, in the sedimentary rock of the racetrack and its walls, that ancient fossils of the legendary Sioux Unkche Ghila have been

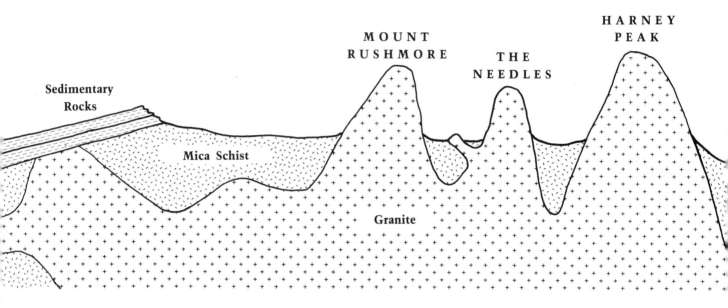

Sedimentary Rocks

MOUNT RUSHMORE

THE NEEDLES

HARNEY PEAK

Mica Schist

Granite

An idealized cross section of the Mount Rushmore area.

found. The fossils, which are preserved remains of animal or plant life, range from tiny sea creatures that lived in the early inland seas millions and millions of years ago, to enormous bones, skulls, and tusks of warm-blooded mammoths that roamed the Black Hills only twenty-six thousand years ago.

The mountains that rise in the center of the Black Hills are composed of igneous granite and the metamorphic mica schist. These rock forms are not as neatly layered as might be expected. Irregular fingers of granite were created when the hot liquid magma flowed up from below and squeezed into the older mica schist before cooling and crystallizing.

In the millions of years that it took for the Black Hills to "uplift" to an elevation of twelve or thirteen thousand feet above sea level, and in the millions of years since it happened, water, wind, and ice have worn away the soft, comparatively young sedimentary rock on top of the mountains. Even the harder mica schist, which can still be seen on the edge of the mountains, has eroded, leaving the heart, the bare, jagged weather-resistant granite peaks, those fingers of cooled magma that are Mount Rushmore, the Needles, Harney Peak, and the other mountains of the Harney Range. As a result of this continuous erosion, which is still going on today, Harney Peak, the highest mountain in the Black Hills, is now only 7242 feet above sea level, with most of the other peaks five to six thousand feet high, thousands of feet lower than when they first uplifted.

The same forces and activity which thrust the Black Hills up into mountains also filled them with precious minerals. Granite itself is a commercial mineral; lithium, beryl, tin, rose quartz, copper, lead, silver, uranium, tourmaline, agate, feldspar, and aquamarine have all been found in the Hills' more than six thousand square miles. But of course, it was the Custer Expedition's discovery of gold in 1874 that lured thousands of white men into the Sioux sacred ground and exploded a few isolated log cabins into rough-and-tumble boom towns like Deadwood, and expanded characters such as Wild Bill Hickok and Calamity Jane into legends. The Homestake Mine in the northwest corner of the Black Hills is the largest underground gold mine in the United States today, as well as the richest.

The same eons of time that formed the Black Hills and their mineral resources also saw the area develop into an isolated island with its own climate and soil. Set apart from the vast sea of Plains grass that surrounds them, the Black Hills are host to plants and animals that mysteriously live together here and nowhere else. Bur oak and American elm from the East exist alongside yucca and cactus from the Southwest, ponderosa pine and Rocky Mountain juniper from the West, and white spruce from the North. There is a mixed range of birds too, with birds such as the indigo bunting and the ovenbird on the very western edge of their range, with others like the mountain bluebird and the western tanager on the very eastern edge.

To add to the mystery, explorers, early mountain men, and Indians all reported strange rumblings and boomings like the roar of a cannon coming from the Black Hills that was definitely not thunder. Although there have been no reports of these loud noises since 1833, no one has ever been able to explain their source satisfactorily.

Unique in its geology, history, resources, and biology, the Black Hills, at the heart of our nation, provide an appropriate setting for a statement about what our country represents. It was a statement that Gutzon Borglum felt qualified to make as he began the task of carving the ancient, weatherworn granite of Mount Rushmore. Did he ever consider the eons of time that it took to create this peak that he was so eager to drill and blast? One wonders.

CHAPTER

· 6 ·

ANXIOUS as Borglum was to begin carving, he had to measure and test the granite first. After the necessary laws were passed to permit the sculpture, he and Major Jesse Tucker, a retired army engineer and Borglum's long-time assistant, spent three days measuring and analyzing the mountain. But Borglum's primary concern during that month of September 1925 was organizing the dedication ceremonies that he had planned for October 1. Always a master promoter, and eager to excite public interest, Borglum staged the dedication like a theatrical production.

The local people must have anticipated a good show. Despite the fact that the roads from Rapid City twenty-five miles away were basically only trails, three thousand spectators turned up, and Borglum didn't disappoint them. Not only were there speeches by Doane Robinson, the originator of the sculpture idea, by Senator Peter Norbeck, who had now become a driving force behind the project, and by Borglum and others, but a band played and a troop of cavalry fired salutes. On top of the mountain, eighteen-by-twenty-four-foot flags were dramatically raised by men dressed in French, Spanish, and English costumes to portray the former owners of the land that historically had encompassed Mount Rushmore.

The Indians, who weren't totally forgotten, were represented by one Sioux brave in full native dress.

A riveting speaker, Borglum was at his best when he promised his audience "the hand of Providence is seen decreeing that a national monument like this shall be erected before a monument shall be erected to any one section [of the nation]." He also promised his listeners that if they came back in a year, they would see the first head finished.

Although the dedication ceremony aroused public interest and even softened up a few hostile newspaper editors, at the end of a year, not only was no head finished, no head was even started. Lack of money was the problem. Throughout 1925, 1926, and most of 1927, almost no contributions came into the treasury of the Mount Harney Memorial Association, that committee of South Dakota businessmen and boosters which had been organized by law in 1925 to control the finances for the sculpture

Raising the French Bourbon flag on top of Mount Rushmore during the October 1, 1925, dedication ceremony.

and oversee the carving. Unfortunately, the law provided no funding, and Borglum's Eastern business friends and other wealthy acquaintances weren't donating the generous sums of money that he kept assuring everyone they would.

Despite the fact that Borglum always had been, and always would be, unrealistic about money, his role in those early years cannot be overemphasized. His dynamic charm, when he chose to use it, and his vitality and drive were what kept the project alive at all. Carving a national monument had now become the motivating force of his life, and his vision and determination, as well as that of Robinson, Norbeck, and South Dakota Congressman William Williamson, at that point, were about all Mount Rushmore had going for it.

And Borglum was nothing if not persistent. With photographs he had taken of the three small model heads he had sculpted of Washington, Jefferson, and Lincoln in 1926, he traveled around the country trying to drum up money and interest, mostly money, in Mount Rushmore. Certainly no one could be more persuasive than Borglum when his conversation sparkled and his full attention was riveted on his listeners. To promote the sculpture project, Borglum even joined Norbeck and Williamson in Washington in an unsuccessful appeal to the federal government for money.

Despite an empty Mount Harney Association treasury, Borglum signed an agreement with the Association in March 1927. Instead of a salary, he was to receive twenty-five percent of all monies spent on labor, materials, and machinery, with the amount not to exceed an overall $87,500. In the agreement, Borglum, as Sculptor, was to be given "full, final and complete freedom and authority" for the monument's "artistic excellence."

At Borglum's insistence, Major Tucker, who was to take care of the day-to-day work, demanded and received a promise of $10,000 a year, an enormous sum in those days. Borglum, who fought for Tucker's high salary, wanted an experienced man in charge at the mountain so that he would be free to travel and work on other sculpture commissions. Even now Borglum was working on other projects, which was fortunate as he was spending his own money promoting Mount Rushmore around the country without as yet having received any salary. And Borglum was a man accustomed to a pleasant and comfortable life-style.

It was during this period, when finances were a critical problem, that Doane Robinson, as secretary of the Mount Harney Association, began to annoy Borglum seriously with his constant harping on cutting costs. Borglum even accused Robinson of lacking courage, a strange accusation to make against one who had single-handedly launched the whole mountain sculpture idea.

At any rate, on May 25, 1927, when the financial picture was at its bleakest, a bonanza fell into Borglum's lap. After much urging from Norbeck and Williamson, President Calvin Coolidge announced that he would be spending a three-month summer vacation at the State Game Lodge in Custer State Park, only a few miles from Rushmore. In his usual theatrical style, Borglum greeted the president's arrival by dropping a wreath of flowers for Mrs. Coolidge on the Lodge lawn from a low-flying airplane.

The president's stay in the Black Hills that summer was a tremendous boost that generated interest in Mount Rushmore, as well as contributions. With a little money in the treasury, Borglum was off and running. Right away, he and Tucker arranged for the permanent loan of a 200-horsepower diesel engine which they housed along with some other machinery in a building they constructed in Keystone, a little mining town three miles away from Mount Rushmore. The diesel engine would generate all the electricity needed to operate the air compressors that would be located at the base of Rushmore.

Once Borglum and Tucker started working, they really hustled. In July they hired sixteen men and bought three air compressors as well as jackhammers, or pneumatic drills, and other equipment. A cut was made through the dense forest between Keystone and Mount Rushmore for the power line, and more trees were felled to open a wagon trail for a team of horses to get through at least partway with the heavy equipment; everything had to be carried by hand the rest of the way.

Daily bulletins at the mountain urged "RUSH MORE," and that was what everyone did. A three-inch air line was laid from the air compressors at the base of the mountain fifteen hundred feet up to the top where it would provide power through pipes to the individual drills. Workers carried up machinery, cement, and lumber, a backbreaking job. Carpenters constructed rough buildings on the top of the mountain and made over an old log cabin slaughterhouse at the base for Borglum to use as a temporary studio. A cookhouse was built, a well was dug for drinking water, and a stream dammed to supply water to cool the compressors.

Borglum had planned an elaborate ceremony for August 10 to celebrate officially the first drilling on Mount Rushmore, with President

President Calvin Coolidge at the dedication of the first drilling, with Borglum (arms folded) seated behind him, August 10, 1927.

Coolidge as the main speaker, and as the date approached, the pace picked up. Seven more men were hired to construct a 760-step stairway up the mountain and to connect the air line to the individual drills.

On August 10, 1927, almost two years after the original flag-raising ceremony, President Calvin Coolidge drove from his summer White House to Keystone; from there, the taciturn Vermont farmboy, self-consciously sporting a ten-gallon hat and cowboy boots, rode by horseback

the rest of the way to the mountain, followed by a grumbling press corps on foot. With no cannon available, Borglum stage-managed an impressive twenty-one-gun presidential salute by blasting out tree stumps where a road would eventually be built.

At the ceremony, presided over by Senator Peter Norbeck, Coolidge and the other guests sat on a makeshift pine platform while 1700 spectators stood or sat where they could find room. Although Charles Rushmore had been invited, he was sick and unable to come, donating instead $5000, one of the largest individual contributions made. When it was the president's turn to speak, he urged public and private support for the project. "This memorial will be another national shrine to which future generations will . . . declare their continuing allegiance to independence, to self government, to freedom and to economic justice." It was the first time the word "shrine" had been used in connection with Mount Rushmore, a term that would eventually expand to "The Shrine of Democracy."

In response, Borglum asked the president to write the inscription which would be carved in the huge entablature next to the four heads on the mountain face, using, naturally, Borglum's own set of historical guidelines. "I want the name Coolidge on that mountain," declared Borglum, never one to pass up an opportunity to enlist support, particularly if that support came from the president of the United States.

Now the moment had arrived. Coolidge handed Borglum four steel drills, and Borglum and Tucker immediately set off to climb the mountain. Seated in a deceptively frail-looking bosun's chair that was actually a sturdy harness made of steel and leather, the dauntless Borglum was lowered over the side of the cliff by Tucker, who was hand-operating a winch from the top of the mountain. Borglum looked tiny up there in the bright August sunlight, and the cable that supported his harness seemed no more than a thread. The crowd held its breath. Suddenly there was a staccato chatter as Borglum began to drill what would someday be Washington's forehead. Hanging there on the side of the mountain, more than likely relishing the excitement he knew he was generating below, Borglum used all four drills.

Upon his descent from the mountain, he symbolically presented the first drill to the president, the second to Senator Norbeck, the third to Doane Robinson, keeping the fourth for himself. It is doubtful that any of those men, even the feisty Borglum, could anticipate the frustrations and difficulties that lay ahead.

DESPITE the ceremonial first drilling in August 1927, Gutzon Borglum had two more months of preparation before he could begin actual work. A whole work-town had to be constructed at the base of the mountain—a blacksmith's shop, tool sheds, compressor houses for the three air compressors, and a bunkhouse for the men, as well as a cableway that would carry tools and equipment up the mountain. On top of the mountain, a network of walkways joined a repair shop, storage sheds for tools and supplies, a small studio, houses for the winches, an office, and a shed to shelter workers from sudden storms.

Despite his apparent self-confidence, Borglum later wrote, "I confess I have never been free from fear and anxiety over the outcome of every phase of the undertaking." Now, with the basic buildings up, he was ready to take his first step in the carving. For his Stone Mountain sculpture, he had projected pictures of his model on the mountain at night, then painted the outline of those pictures on the rock. But the granite of Rushmore was too rough and imperfect to predict ahead of time exactly where the heads could be located, and until the outer flawed rock was removed to expose the granite underneath, Borglum had no way of knowing what the quality of the rock would be, making projections impractical.

Even though he had been warned by a geologist that the fissures were quite deep, Borglum announced that he wouldn't have to use dynamite as he had on Stone Mountain. However, when he started working and realized that there was no way he could reach solid, crack-free rock without it, he had to swallow his words, and by the time the four heads were finished, ninety percent of all stone removed had been dynamited off, a total of 450,000 tons, almost four times as much as Borglum had originally estimated. "We have literally carved with dynamite," he later commented.

As soon as Borglum decided on the approximate position of each head, men were lowered down the mountain in harnesses to drill holes for the dynamite charges. The harnesses, which Borglum had designed for Stone Mountain, were constructed of a leather-covered steel frame that looked like a bosun's chair. Two tugs that were actually leather straps went along the side of the arms, with a leather belt that fastened around the worker's waist and another belt that came up between his legs, so that even if he were unconscious, he couldn't fall out. The harness, which gave a worker great mobility on the mountain, was connected to a hand-operated winch located in a winch house on top of the mountain by a flexible steel cable three-eighths of an inch thick.

Winch men hand-operate the winches that raise and lower workers in their harnesses and swinging cages.

For the drilling, the men used air-powered jackhammers, weighing anywhere from twenty to sixty-five pounds, which were snapped to a chain on the spreader bar of the harness so that the worker wouldn't have to carry the weight of the heavy drill when he was lowered by cable down the mountain face. The jackhammer was in the shape of a T and when the worker started drilling, he braced his foot against the mountain and steadied the drill against his instep until the bit had rotated into the rock half an inch or so. Air was supplied to the individual drills by rubber hoses which were connected to the air line that ran to the top of the mountain from the electrically powered air compressors at the base.

A basic rule was that when the surface that the driller wanted to reach was twenty feet or more deep in the rock, the holes for the dynamite would be about eight or nine feet deep, one and a half to two feet apart, in a line of fifteen to twenty holes. The jackhammers were equipped with four-star drill bits, and an experienced driller, with a sixty-pound jackhammer and a new drill bit, could drill a foot and a half a minute. The more pressure he exerted, the faster he drilled. Depending on how hard the rock was, the drill bits had to be replaced after drilling an average of only three feet.

Because a driller was suspended in his harness for four hours at a time, and because the drill bits ranged from a few inches to many feet in length, he couldn't possibly carry fresh bits with him, so when his bit dulled, he signaled for a replacement. Lowered down in his own harness, a man known as a steel monkey would exchange the driller's dull bit for a fresh bit from the big leather pouch he carried on his shoulder. The old bit was then sent down by cable car to the blacksmith's shop at the base of the mountain, where it was heated, sharpened, tempered, and sent back up the mountain to be used again. The blacksmith sharpened several hundred four-star drill bits a day just to keep the drilling crews supplied.

A go-between known as a call boy kept the driller in touch with the steel monkey, as well as with the winch men up above who hand-operated a bank of six or seven winches in the winch house. Stationed on the face of the mountain and securely fastened to a cable, the call boy could see both the drillers in their harnesses and the winch house up above. Each harness had a number, so when a worker wanted to be raised or lowered he would signal the call boy, who in turn would relay the message "Eight Up" or "Eight Down" over his microphone to the loudspeaker in the winch house. There the winch men would hand-lower or hand-raise that particular harness on its 300-foot-long cable accordingly.

A call boy waits to relay orders from the drillers to the winch men on top of the mountain.

OPPOSITE: Thousands of feet above sea level, a worker in his leather and steel harness drills holes for the dynamite charges.

5 7

After the holes were drilled, the drillers were raised up the mountain in their harnesses, and the powder men, or powder monkeys as they were sometimes called, would be lowered down in similar harnesses to place their charges of dynamite. After loading two or three sticks of dynamite in each hole, they wired all the blasting caps together in a series and packed the holes with wet sand to protect the remaining rock from the jarring effect of the blast. After running the electrical wire that connected the caps up the mountain, they detonated the charges electrically either at noon when everyone was eating lunch on top of the mountain, or at 4 P.M. after the men had left work for the day.

Although it wasn't always possible, Borglum liked to take off the outer rock in such a way that the surface would be a rough, egg-shaped mass. Then, if he came upon flawed rock, he could change the position of the head he was carving, even moving the center of the face or the nose ten feet one way or the other if he had to. Borglum was always careful not to make any indentations for the face's features until he was certain the rock was crack-free.

As more and more rock was removed, and as the egg shape began to emerge, the men drilled the holes for the dynamite shallower and closer together, using less powder for the blasting. In some cases, when the rock

Powder men place dynamite charges in the drill holes.

was six or eight inches from the final working surface, and the holes were drilled as close together as possible, the men would pop off the rock using only the mercury blasting cap without any dynamite. Although the powder men became so skillful they could dynamite within an inch or two of the working surface, they usually left an extra three to six inches of rock. Any closer than that and the charges would have had to be so small and the holes so close together that neither time nor labor would have been saved. Furthermore, for obvious reasons, it was better to remove too little rock than too much.

When the oval mass of the face was shaped to Borglum's satisfaction, he was ready for the next stage of the carving, a technique known as pointing, which he had also used on Stone Mountain. Borglum had already made plaster models of the heads in his studio that were scaled on a ratio of one to twelve, with one inch on the studio models expanding to twelve inches on the mountain. The heads, which were five feet from chin to forehead in the studio, would measure 60 feet on the mountain, with eyes that would be 11 feet across, a nose 20 feet long, and a mouth 18 feet wide. The sculpture was 365 feet across at its widest point, with the distance from the top of the heads to the bottom of the coats measuring 160 feet. If the figures were full-length, they would be 465 feet tall!

Starting with the head of Washington, Borglum centered a circular plate marked off in degrees from zero to 360 on the top of the studio model head. Fastened to the center of the plate was a horizontal beam like a yardstick marked out in feet and inches that could swing in an arc, with a steel weight known as a plumb bob hanging down from the beam by a steel wire. Using this pointing machine, Borglum swung the beam out over Washington's nose, the feature that projected out the farthest. He then measured the two distances, the horizontal distance along the beam, and the vertical distance from the beam down to where the plumb bob touched the nose, also noting the precise degree at which the beam was angled on the circular plate.

Borglum, who had already located where the top and center of Washington's head would be on the mountain, bolted to that spot a circular plate marked off in degrees that was exactly like the circular plate in the studio, only twelve times larger. Attached to the plate like a mast was an upright shaft which supported and kept level a thirty-foot horizontal swinging movable boom that was marked off in feet and inches. The boom, which was actually a steel I-beam, projected out over the face of the mountain. Suspended from the boom by steel piano wires were two plumb bobs that operated on a track by pulleys. These plumb bobs could be hung anywhere along the length of the boom, while the piano wires, marked with measurements, could be dropped to any desired length by a device mounted on the boom that resembled a fishing reel.

First the degree reading on the circular plate on top of the studio head was duplicated on the circular plate on top of the mountain so that the steel boom could be swung to exactly the same angle. Then both the horizontal and vertical measurements taken in the studio were duplicated on the mountain by multiplying the figures by twelve.

The pointing machine on top of the head guarantees accurate measurements on the mountain face. Vertical lines indicate where rock has already been blasted off as workers drill for more dynamiting.

Using these figures to adjust the position of the boom and the plumb bob that was nearest the mountain, Borglum was now able to touch the mountain face with the plumb bob exactly where the tip of Washington's nose should be. A second plumb bob of the same length hung two feet farther out on the boom so that the driller could line up the two plumb bobs, allowing him to drill into the mountain at a straight angle.

After the contours of Washington's face had been measured out on the mountain, those measured points were painted in blocks of a square foot each, with a number to indicate how deep the driller should drill that particular block. For instance, when Washington's nose was located on the mountain by the plumb bob, a circle with a red dot in the center was painted on the rock, with *No. 1, 6'* painted beside the circle to indicate that six feet of stone needed to be removed at that particular location.

When Borglum wanted even more precise detail work, he had the points made closer together until they were only two or three inches apart. The plaster casts that he had made of the individual studio heads, called sectional molds, were taken up the mountain so that accurate measurements could be transferred directly onto the faces. Borglum used this pointing technique on all four heads with the workmen in charge of the pointing machine known as pointers. Because he was responsible for making the precise measurements, as well as approving all drilling and blasting, the pointer, next to the Sculptor, was the most important man on the mountain.

For the next step, the semi-finishing work, Borglum built scaffoldings of heavy bridge timbers in eight-foot stories that were bolted to lumps of rock left projecting from the mountain face and reinforced with steel. From these scaffoldings, which sometimes ran the whole width of the face, the men drilled *vertical* holes one and a half to two feet deep every two or three inches at a depth indicated by the painted points.

With the granite thus weakened by the vertical holes, the men used a unique tool called a channel iron. Run by an air drill like a jackhammer, the channel iron was a flat piece of steel one and a half to two feet long, three or four inches wide, and one-half inch thick, with a serrated cutting edge like a saw. The channel iron, which hammered rather than rotated like the jackhammer, cut out the web between the row of holes like a saw, creating a deep trench in the rock about one and a half to two feet deep. It was then easy to pry off the block of granite with a steel wedge, one of the few steps in the entire carving process done by hand.

Now the wooden scaffolding was removed, and the one-foot-square

A worker wedges off sections of
rock by hand after the channel
iron has weakened it.

lumps of rock used to anchor the scaffolding were chiseled off. One such
eighteen-inch lump of rock on Washington's jaw that can be seen from
the air but not from the ground was never removed, either intentionally
or by accident.

Although scaffolding made a steadier and more convenient platform on which to stand, for the final finishing work, when Borglum needed an unobstructed view of the faces in order to make final artistic decisions, the men worked from movable cages that could be raised or lowered out of sight by cable. A two-man cage was eight feet long by four feet wide, and was attached to the winch house on top of the mountain by two cables, while a one-man cage, four feet by four feet, was suspended by a single cable. On occasion, the cages, like the scaffoldings, were anchored to lumps of rock in order to free the cable and winch apparatus for more harnesses.

Up until this time, ninety percent of the work had been engineering, the removal of unwanted granite, but the last ten percent of the carving, those final two or three inches that gave the sculpture its life and vitality, was strictly an artistic effort. Borglum could get within one-quarter inch accuracy from the models onto the mountain, but because of light and shadow, perspective, angle, and distance, all factors not present in the studio, his artist's eye was essential for seeing what changes needed to be made on the site.

He observed the mountain at dawn, in the bright sun, at dusk, in the fog and rain, and from every possible angle, even through binoculars from Iron Mountain four miles away, constantly analyzing the play of light and shadow. He turned Washington's head twenty degrees farther south to allow the sun to light the north side of the face until the early afternoon. He also recessed the pupils of Lincoln's eyes to permit a twenty-two-inch shaft to protrude that would give the eye a lifelike expression. Because of all these on-the-spot changes, the four completed heads on the mountain could never be considered exact copies of the studio models.

Actually, Borglum had never intended his finished sculpture to be a duplication of the models. He believed "that sculpture or art of any kind that is developed in the small design model and from that literally enlarged mechanically, is lifeless, bloodless. . . . It is lifeless because it is not struggled over in the making *full size*, but simply copied. . . . I believe every bit of art that hopes to be great must be fought with creative effort in its final size."

For that critical finishing work, Borglum was lowered down the mountain in a harness to indicate with red paint what feature he wanted to emphasize or what line needed softening. Although a quick change was easily made on the studio model, it took three or four days for a driller to make the same correction on the mountain.

Using the painted points as a guide, the workmen now drilled a series

A harness, a swinging cage, and two-story scaffolding are often in use at the same time.

of holes horizontally into the rock close together and only two or three inches deep, a process that was called honeycombing because of the honeycomb effect it produced. Either the honeycombed sections were knocked off by the sharp-pointed bit of a drill known as a plugger, or they were taken off by hand with a mallet and chisel.

But honeycombing left the granite pockmarked with drill holes and ridges like the surface of a golf ball. To achieve a smooth surface, the men used small, easily controlled air guns called bumpers that bounced up and down on the rock flaking off small shards and leaving the final surface as smooth as a concrete sidewalk. Because the bumper vibrated even more than a jackhammer, its four-cornered facing bit, with two sharp triangle-shaped impressions, needed constant resharpening. Not only did this finishing work demand skill on the part of the worker, but it also required Borglum's being constantly available to supervise exactly how much rock to bump off and where.

To evaluate the carvings means to consider them in artistic terms, and it is true that Borglum agonized for years over the four heads, their features, their expressions, their angles, as well as their arrangement in an eye-pleasing unit. But it is also true that the carvings are an amazing feat of engineering. Although Borglum's Stone Mountain experience had been a failure, he later admitted that if he had not perfected certain engineering techniques on Stone Mountain, he could never have tackled Mount Rushmore. With no blueprints or precedents to follow, Borglum, using those procedures he had personally developed, single-handedly transformed a seamed mountain of granite into an awesome national monument.

A bumper smooths the surface of Lincoln's eye. The twenty-two-inch protruding shaft catches the light and gives expression to the face.

OPPOSITE: Working from a movable cage, a driller honeycombs the rock so that it can be wedged off easily.

CHAPTER

· 8 ·

T H A N K S to national news coverage of President Coolidge's visit in 1927, the country was suddenly aware of Mount Rushmore and the beauty of the Black Hills, publicity neither Gutzon Borglum nor the Black Hills community could have bought for any price. And it didn't hurt that the president boasted about the wonderful fishing, his private trout stream having been generously stocked before his arrival.

The donations that came in following the dedication kept work going from October until early December 1927, the only period at Rushmore when Borglum kept a detailed account of day-to-day progress. The first entry, October 4, recorded a memorable moment with a brief, "Today we started the actual drilling on Rushmore." For the next two months, five or six drillers operated at all times, blasting and drilling away the rock to a depth of about twenty-five feet, from the top of Washington's forehead down to where his eyes would be.

On December 7, when the temperature dropped to twenty-two below zero, all work stopped, with the comment in Borglum's black notebook explaining, "Operations shut down because of severe cold and exhausted funds." Traditionally, a work season began in April or May and continued into late fall when the freezing weather made conditions on the mountain hazardous and difficult. Unfortunately, along with the temperature that December, the flow of donations had frozen up too, and with no more money coming in, Borglum had to close down completely.

That first season was a foretaste of problems to come. Borglum charged Doane Robinson and the Mount Harney Association with blocking progress by interfering in his artistic decisions, and there were incessant arguments about money. "I have had two months of mental distress over it," Borglum complained. In reply, Robinson accused Borglum of "belly-aching."

Even more serious than the disagreements was the fact that the project was at a complete standstill. With Borglum's unfinished Stone Mountain sculpture fresh in everyone's mind, and with no work being done on Rushmore, people were reluctant to contribute. Only hard work by Senator Peter Norbeck and Representative William Williamson at this point saved the sculpture from going under forever. In 1929 they maneuvered Public Law 805 through Congress that replaced the old Mount Harney Memorial Association with the new Mount Rushmore National Memorial Commission. The commission was composed of twelve members appointed by President Coolidge in one of his last acts as president.

The law granted $250,000 for the sculpture on a matching-fund basis, which meant that the government would match dollar-for-dollar all the money that the new commission raised. That, of course, presented the commissioners with the immediate problem of raising money for the government to match. The law also stated that no admission should ever be charged to see the newly named Mount Rushmore National Memorial, a title and a policy that have lasted to this day.

At least the passage of the bill meant that the government would now match what the old Mount Harney Association had spent, a total of $55,000, and with that amount Borglum was able to start up work again in June 1929, a year and a half after it had been suspended. And he had a new log cabin studio at the base of Doane Mountain in which to work that gave him a perfect view of Rushmore just a quarter of a mile away across a canyon. Named after Doane Robinson, Doane Mountain has always been the traditional area from which to view the sculpture.

Beginning where they left off in 1927, Borglum, Tucker, and their crew carved down from Washington's eyebrows to the end of his chin, working on all his features. By now, Borglum had decided to place Jefferson slightly lower than Washington and on his right, with Lincoln on Washington's left, and Roosevelt to the left of Lincoln. By the end of the

1929 work season, Washington's forehead, starting at the hairline, was almost done, and his eyebrows, eyelids, eyeballs, and nose were all drilled to within a couple of inches of where the final finished surface would be.

Unfortunately, when the new commission, especially John A. Boland, chairman of the executive committee who was in charge of finances, took a look at the budget, it decided that Major Tucker's $10,000-a-year salary was excessive and refused to pay Tucker what was still owed him or take over his earlier contract with the Mount Harney Association. Furious with the decision, Tucker quit. Borglum, who had been leaving the daily supervision of Mount Rushmore to Tucker while he worked on other sculptures in his San Antonio, Texas, studio, appointed J. C. Denison as the new superintendent in 1929. But Denison was inexperienced and Borglum knew it.

"When Mr. Tucker left, there was no saving the monument or the project except by my assuming all responsibility. I did that and I have done it to this moment; I expect to do it until the end of the work," Borglum wrote. Anticipating his new role, Borglum bought a three thousand-acre ranch near Hermosa, South Dakota, only twenty miles from Rushmore, where he lived for the rest of his life, traveling with his family to Texas only when Rushmore closed down for the winter.

Borglum made good progress in 1929, but when 1930 came around the money had dried up again. Being inventive, if nothing else, Borglum put together a brochure about Mount Rushmore which generated national publicity, as well as $10,000, which totaled $20,000 when the government matched the amount. That same year, the commission formed the Mount Rushmore National Memorial Society, a booster club with individual memberships at $100, thus raising, with matching funds, an additional $11,000.

These campaigns brought in enough money to get the work going full steam ahead for the dedication of the Washington head, which Borglum was determined to hold on July 4, 1930, no matter what stage of completion the Washington head was in. Most of that spring's efforts were concentrated on finishing work on Washington, as well as dynamiting off some of the remaining stone beside the head to set it off to better advantage. Borglum also roughed out Jefferson's features to the right of Washington, as well as the beginning of the first line of the entablature, *1776*, on Washington's far left.

It was at this point that Calvin Coolidge again entered the picture. At the original dedication in 1927, Borglum had asked the president to write

a brief history of the United States to be carved into the mountain. Using Borglum's set of historical guidelines, Coolidge, who was no longer president, had now completed the task, but when he submitted the first part of his essay, Borglum rewrote it to suit himself. Coolidge was understandably irritated, particularly since the press got wind of the changes and endlessly criticized both versions, making its own suggestions as to what historical events should be included and how they should be written.

Scaffolding covers Washington, with rock removed on his right for Jefferson and on his far left for the entablature.

7 1

The situation between Coolidge and Borglum became so heated, it was reported that during the controversy, Coolidge asked how far his Massachusetts home was from Mount Rushmore and when told the distance was two thousand miles, he replied, "that is just about as close to Mr. Borglum as I want to be." Borglum's high-handed approach offended countless numbers of people over the years, but never did he offend such a famous person so publicly.

But again, high-handed or not, the Borglum–Coolidge conflict gave the memorial an enormous amount of newspaper publicity, and now that the state of South Dakota had built a road from Rapid City to Keystone, with another road from Keystone to the base of the mountain, tourists began to find their way to Rushmore. Although the sculpture has brought in many millions of tourist dollars to the state over the years, the $2,000,000 South Dakota paid for the roads within a fifteen-mile radius of Rushmore is the only money the state ever spent on the project, a fact that Borglum always resented.

In the early months of the 1930 work season, about four hundred tourists a day were arriving at Borglum's studio on Doane Mountain to watch him work. Being an actor at heart, Borglum dressed dramatically in a business suit and Stetson hat with a wide scarf around his neck to put on his usual performance. When prominent visitors were expected, Borglum would sometimes go up the mountain and dangle off the rock face in a harness, an impressive sight indeed.

And then it was July 4, 1930, and although the Washington head was far from completed, it was time for the dedication. Because of the unpredictable nature of the granite, Borglum never finished one head before starting another. Until he began drilling, he wasn't able to anticipate where one head would finally fit in best to blend artistically with the others. Nevertheless, finished or not, Borglum, with his intuitive sense of timing, realized that with money again running out, he needed to put Rushmore before the public eye again.

And he staged his usual professional production. With Jefferson's rough features and the numbers *1776* visible on either side of Washington, the face was covered throughout the ceremony by a huge, seventy-two-by-forty-foot American flag sewn by a group of Rapid City women.

In his opening speech, Joseph S. Cullinan, chairman of the Mount Rushmore National Memorial Commission, spoke of Mount Rushmore as "America's Shrine for Political Democracy," repeating the word "shrine" that Calvin Coolidge had first used back in 1927, a word that has

Men in movable cages do final finishing work on Washington.

come to be an accepted part of Rushmore's title. Dr. Cleophas O'Harra, president of the South Dakota School of Mines, and Doane Robinson also spoke, with Dr. O'Harra answering his own question as to how long the sculpture would last. "One hundred years? Yes. One thousand years? Yes. A hundred thousand years? In all likelihood, yes. A half million years? Possibly so, nobody knows."

Gutzon Borglum concluded the speeches with the claim that "the great face [Washington's] seemed to belong to the mountain; it took on the elemental courage of the mountains surrounding it." What Borglum meant by that was never quite clear, but it had the ring of grandeur about it, and that was enough for the twenty-five hundred enthusiastic spectators as the huge American flag over Washington's face was pulled aside to the accompaniment of rifles firing and airplanes roaring overhead.

The national publicity given to the dedication had a few mixed reviews, with several critics again taking Borglum to task. "The mountain . . . is a kind of earth sculpture of its own and loses its intrinsic majesty and dignity when man uses it as a bill board," wrote the art critic for the Detroit *News.*

During that same month, Borglum replaced Denison, who predictably lasted only a year as superintendent, with former pointer William Tallman, a long-time friend and competent young artist who had studied with Borglum as a boy. Borglum also hired Hugo Villa, an Italian sculptor with whom he had worked for fourteen years on other projects.

And then, only three weeks after the festive Washington dedication, funds again ran out. With clear-eyed hindsight, the commission realized that instead of simply being satisfied with whatever money came in, it should have launched an aggressive fund-raising drive early in 1929 when money was plentiful and the country was in a free-spending mood. Nine months before, on Black Thursday, October 24, 1929, the stock market had collapsed, bringing the nation's economy down with it.

Certainly during such a crisis there was little interest in the financial problems of a remote mountain sculpture. "We lost the finest opportunity we had," Representative Williamson lamented as the country entered the deepest and longest financial depression in its history, a depression that lasted throughout all the remaining Rushmore years.

I T was unfortunate that money was always such a critical issue. Borglum was at his best when funds were available for work, when no one, especially the Memorial Commission's John Boland, was pressing him to cut costs, and when his own financial picture was bright. Reinforcing his concern in having work continue on the mountain was the fact that his "salary," the twenty-five percent of all monies spent on the sculpture, was based entirely on the amount of funds put into the project. Unquestionably, Borglum was at his worst when the commission, under John Boland, was pulling the purse strings tight.

At least the pressure was off Doane Robinson. Although he was a member of the new Mount Rushmore National Memorial Commission, he was no longer responsible for the monument's finances. John Boland, who had taken over that difficult role, was now in charge of raising money and making sure it was wisely spent. He also had the thankless task of having to deal with Borglum's financial irresponsibility.

Senator Norbeck once said, "There will never be a Rushmore Memorial completed if Borglum is permitted to handle the business end of it." And it was true that right from the start, Borglum seemed incapable of staying within a budget or being practical in any way about money.

Whenever he got involved in finances, which was often, there was trouble. There had been trouble with the old Mount Harney Association, trouble with Doane Robinson, trouble with Congress, and now there was trouble with John Boland and the commission.

And of course, funds, or the lack of funds, affected the workers too. When there was money coming in, seventy men might work at the same time; when money was scarce, Borglum might get down to as few as one to four men; and when there was no money at all, the carving closed down completely. Although Borglum worked on Mount Rushmore for fourteen years, from 1927 to 1941, because of all the shutdowns that resulted from lack of funds, the actual time he and his men spent carving totaled only six and a half years.

Most of the workers were local unemployed loggers, ranchers, or miners whom Borglum trained on the site, with only a few skilled stone carvers ever on the job. After all, where could Borglum find men trained to operate sixty-pound jackhammers while swinging in a harness two hundred feet in the air? A definite plus was that many of the powder men were former hard-rock miners from the nearby closed-down Holy Terror Gold Mine who were expert in the use of dynamite.

At one time or another, 360 men worked on the mountain, some of them returning year after year, especially after 1931, when the country was locked into the Depression. With only about a hundred men working those last ten years, from 1931 to 1941, the crew became a close-knit group, even forming an enthusiastic baseball team. An average of thirty men worked at one time, usually for the regular spring-through-fall season. Under the best of circumstances, there would be one or two pointers on the mountain, the foreman, two to four winch men, a steel monkey, and as many drillers as Borglum could afford.

The workday, which began at 7:30 A.M. with an exhausting half-hour climb up the long stairway to the top of the heads, ended at 4 P.M. Throughout the Rushmore years, the pay scale varied according to the skill required for the job. In the early years, drillers were paid 50¢ to 60¢ an hour, while the few trained carvers earned $1 an hour. By the late 1930s, unskilled workers might earn 50¢ to 60¢ an hour, drillers 75¢ an hour, powder men $1, carvers $1.25, with the master pointer earning $1.55 an hour; all of which was not bad considering this was during a time when the country's unemployment rate went over twenty-five percent. With the national economy at rock bottom, it was no wonder that the workmen were eager to return every year, dangerous conditions or not, and as the features of the four presidents began to emerge, part of that eagerness stemmed from pride in what they were accomplishing as well.

Of course a job on Mount Rushmore meant working with Borglum. Like everyone else who had to deal with him, the men often found Borglum, whom they usually called "The Chief," unpredictable and difficult, and it was fatal to disagree with him. One long-time worker commented, "If the Old Man said it was going to rain and the sun was shining, I said, 'It sure looks like rain.'"

Borglum, in turn, observed, "If my men do not follow them [my plans], they have got to have better ways or good reasons or they take a holiday."

Although one of the carvers held a record for being fired and rehired eight times, most of the men eventually learned to adjust to Borglum's temperament, and in the long run, came to respect his determination to see the project through *his* way, as well as realizing that he would never ask them to do anything he wouldn't do himself. A winch and a swing harness were reserved for Borglum at all times on the top of each head. "In all serious matters affecting design, I go down," Borglum wrote in 1930, "or we [he and his assistants] may all go down and there on the side of the mountain sit in our swings and hold conferences regarding any problem in hand."

And Borglum gave more of himself than just time and talent. When work shut down after the Washington dedication in July 1930, he bought five memberships in the Mount Rushmore National Memorial Society at $100 each and donated $1500. That same year, the commission launched a campaign to raise dimes and quarters from South Dakota schoolchildren with the hope that the idea would spread to other states, which, unfortunately, it never did.

At any rate, what money did come in, combined with Borglum's personal contributions, was matched by government funds, and the total amounted to enough for Borglum to start up work again on August 15 and continue until November 6, 1930. Consumed as Borglum was with Rushmore, he could never understand the commission's inability to raise the money needed to match the more than $170,000 the government still held in its matching-fund account. "It seems equally hard to believe that they should allow me to carry the burdens," he protested.

When the 1931 work season opened, the commission had only a ridiculous $10.65 on hand, with Borglum again bailing out the project

A harness is reserved on top of each head for Borglum (center), who checks all phases of work.

with another contribution, this time for $5000. When the commissioners themselves reluctantly pledged money too, Borglum was able to start up work on June 5, although he was still making statements such as "About money for Jefferson—I've got all the big dem's [Democrats] on the carpet and they will I'm sure raise me $135,000 for Jefferson." Although Borglum had been promising for years that his wealthy and influential friends would contribute enough to finance the whole project, it was at last beginning to dawn on the commission that these impressive sums weren't about to materialize soon.

Early in June 1931, Borglum left for Poland to attend an unveiling of his statue of Woodrow Wilson, and he didn't return until late August. Essential to Rushmore in his absence was John Boland's determination to keep the work going. Afraid that if it shut down for lack of funds, it would never start up again, Boland miraculously kept the project alive. "How he keeps the till filled enough to pay the workmen, God knows, I don't," Doane Robinson commented in a local newspaper.

Equally important to the sculpture was the progress that Tallman and Villa made during those two months, with the blasting started in preparation for work on Lincoln, and eight drillers working full-time on Jefferson's features. Whether the extraordinary progress was due to the volatile Borglum's absence or to the fact that the workers were at last becoming skilled at their unusual and hazardous jobs is not certain, but what is certain is that two weeks after Borglum returned in August, he fired Villa.

Although a salary dispute was given as the reason, the clash between Borglum and Villa was more a matter of different artistic philosophies than anything else. Villa strongly believed, and stated in a letter to the governor of South Dakota, that Borglum's studio model didn't fit the existing rock and there wasn't enough room on Washington's right side for Jefferson. Furthermore, Villa pointed out, Borglum was spending entirely too much time away from Rushmore. "I've never been criticized in my life by competent people, either here or abroad, never," Borglum observed to John Boland after firing Villa.

Despite the controversy, progress continued, although by the end of the 1931 work season, on October 1, Borglum was still having problems positioning the four heads. He moved Lincoln farther over to free more of Washington, but he wasn't satisfied with the way that Jefferson and Lincoln seemed to be crowding Washington, almost leaning against him. Back in his studio on Doane Mountain, Borglum kept reworking the

Jefferson, on Washington's right, is already blocked out, as work continues on the entablature to Washington's far left.

ELEVATION
ONE MILE ABOVE
SEA LEVEL

VIEW
MONUMENT
FROM STUDIO
300 FEET
GOOD TRAIL
INFORMATION & SOUVENIRS

location of the heads on his studio model, still undecided as to where he should place Roosevelt.

The following year, 1932, was in Borglum's, and everyone else's, opinion a complete waste. No money in the commission treasury meant no work on the mountain. Even a mailing of form letters requesting one-dollar donations lost money instead of earning it. Borglum was understandably frustrated by John Boland and by the commission's failure to raise funds. "I am utterly sick of the do-nothing policy that we have allowed for three years," he complained.

Again it was Senator Norbeck who saved the day, this time by wangling a government loan to South Dakota under an unemployment relief program which granted $50,000 to Mount Rushmore to hire unemployed workers. Now out-of-work miners were put to work blasting, while about fifty unemployed men were hired to landscape the grounds that now had to accommodate the 100,000 tourists who were visiting Rushmore every year. When Norbeck again stepped in and saw to it that the government matched the $50,000 with an additional $50,000, Mount Rushmore's finances turned the corner, and the situation was never quite so desperate again.

W I T H the welcome arrival of federal funds, carving began on March 24, 1933, and continued straight on through December 10, when the weather turned too cold to work. Although Borglum was gone about half the time, just as he was throughout all the Rushmore years, on speaking tours, trying to raise money, and working on other sculpture commissions, he forwarded constant directions by letter and telegram.

Enormous progress was made during the 1933 season, with tons of rock blasted off from the left side of Washington's wig, the top of his left shoulder, and his chest, and refining work done on his features and his coat lapels. With the completion of the scenic Iron Mountain Road designed by Senator Norbeck that approached Mount Rushmore from the southeast, and with a good graded and graveled road between Rapid City and Mount Rushmore that was finished that summer, more and more tourists were arriving, at least 135,000 in 1933.

What didn't go well for Borglum that season was work on the Jefferson head. He knew he was in trouble as he drilled and blasted ninety feet into the mountain trying to find usable granite, but he postponed making a drastic decision.

Unknown to Borglum, at about that same time, another kind of decision was being made in Washington, one that would have far-reaching effects on both Borglum and Mount Rushmore. Anticipating Borglum's violent reaction, Senator Norbeck delayed telling him the news, that President Franklin D. Roosevelt had decided to place the Mount Rushmore National Memorial under the supervision of the National Park Service in the Department of the Interior—another ironic link with the Sioux. Since 1849, the Bureau of Indian Affairs had been under the supervision of the Department of the Interior, a department historically so corrupt and unprincipled that it had sunk the Indian to a level of poverty that was scandalous even by Depression standards. It wasn't until Harold Ickes became Secretary of the Interior in 1933 that the Department was finally reformed.

What the new supervision meant for Rushmore was that all federal money coming in would have to pass through the National Park Service for examination, although the commission would still remain basically in charge. As it turned out, neither Secretary Ickes, who compared the carving of a mountain to the carving of one's initials on a tree, nor the Park Service was all that pleased to be involved. "Under the policy that has grown up with the National Park Service deliberate inclusion of elaborate works of man has been strenuously opposed," commented the director of the Park Service. It was a statement that didn't bode well for a future working relationship with Borglum, whose whole life was now consumed by his "elaborate works of man" on Mount Rushmore.

For the time being, the Park Service didn't make any immediate changes, which was fortunate for Borglum because when the 1934 season opened on June 15, he was having enough trouble positioning the four heads, particularly Jefferson's. With insufficient stone, and a large crack between Jefferson and Washington, Jefferson's head on Washington's right just wasn't working out. Now Borglum had to face the fact that his assistant Hugo Villa, whom he had since rehired to work in his studio, had been right three years before when he had said that the rock to the right of Washington would never be suitable for Jefferson.

That summer, with what must have been a combination of regret and embarrassment, Borglum ordered the Jefferson head blown off. As the shattered rock tumbled down the mountain, more than $10,000 of labor, materials, and time went with it.

An instant public outcry followed the expensive demolition. It was the old problem of the public, Congress, and even the commission not understanding that until the rock was drilled and blasted, Borglum could not know what kind of granite he would be dealing with, or whether it would even turn out to be usable.

So far, Borglum had shifted the heads around on his studio model seven times so they would conform to the rock he was uncovering in his blasting and drilling. Constantly frustrated by everyone's inability to sympathize with the difficulties of mountain carving, he said that it was "practically impossible to prepare and complete a fixed or final model which could be followed. . . . The design of this colossal work is subject to constant changes as the uncovering of the stone progresses." When he moved Washington's shoulder back fourteen feet to improve his position, it changed the look of Washington so much, people were horrified, thinking he had moved the whole figure.

Fortunately for Borglum, his decision to move Jefferson turned out to be a good one. With Jefferson gone, the Washington head now stood out in bold relief, solitary, prominent, just the way Borglum had envisioned it all along. Now too, the afternoon sun could shine past Washington to light up the rest of the sculpture. Immediately Borglum put most of the thirty men he had hired for the 1934 season, including thirteen drillers, to work on the new Jefferson head on Washington's left, with four to six men working on Washington's collar and his left shoulder and arm.

But when drilling started, Jefferson's new position presented a new problem. A crack ran through his nose, a projecting feature which could easily break off if moisture collected in the crack, froze, and split the rock. Borglum said, "I have no intention of leaving a head on that mountain that in the course of 500 or 5,000 years will be without a nose."

With the old Jefferson blasted off, the new Jefferson takes shape on Washington's left.

Although relocating Jefferson took up at least a third of the time spent on the Jefferson head that summer, the second move wasn't as dramatic as the initial demolition. This time it simply meant shifting the measuring device a matter of feet to a different position on top of the Jefferson studio model, as well as on top of Jefferson's head on the mountain. Finally, Borglum was able to report, "I reset the head five degrees to the north, set it back four feet, then tilted the head about 18 inches."

The crack now ran through Jefferson's right eye, past his nose and upper lip, and through the middle of his chin. Unlike the nose, the face had the bulk of the mountain behind it, so after the crack was sealed with a mixture of equal parts of granite dust and white lead with enough linseed oil to make a paste there would be no chance of its breaking off. Luigi Del Bianco, one of the best stonecutters Rushmore ever had, patched the crack in Jefferson's lip with a foot-deep piece of granite held in place by pins—the only patch on the whole sculpture, and one that is hard to detect even close up.

The fact that so much time and money were spent on blasting off the old Jefferson head and relocating the new one didn't sit well with John Boland, who was strictly a budget-and-schedule man. After working together for five years, Borglum and Boland, who was still chairman of the commission's executive committee, were now waging a running battle over almost every issue, from hiring and salary practices to purchasing equipment, although their basic disagreement concerned which of them was in charge of the finances for the project. The two men, who had to work so closely together, were complete opposites: Borglum was an impulsive individualist, determined to have his own way in every phase of the sculpture, and John Boland was an efficient and exacting businessman who operated strictly by the book.

Borglum, always a prolific writer, kept up a steady correspondence with just about everyone he knew, including President Roosevelt, complaining that Boland was meddling in artistic decisions and slowing down work on the mountain with his constant interference. Boland, on the other hand, was just as stubborn as Borglum about insisting that it was the commission's duty to be in control of all administrative and financial matters. An exasperated Senator Norbeck joined the fray, writing to Borglum in 1934, "You are so deficient in business judgment as to be almost blind."

By 1935, there was so much friction between Borglum and Boland that Boland commented, "I couldn't sleep nights. Borglum was driving

me crazy." Borglum's superintendent of five years, William Tallman, sided with Boland on almost every issue, or at least it seemed that way to Borglum, and Tallman's "disloyalty," whether real or imagined, so aggravated Borglum, Tallman finally resigned. In his 1935 resignation letter, he wrote, "He [Borglum] accused me of being so friendly with Mr. John A. Boland, whom he believes to be working against him, that he cannot trust me."

But controversy never prevented Borglum from making progress on the sculpture, and from June to November of 1935, he supervised about fifty men in the drilling and blasting away of thousands of tons of rock. Not much was done that season to Washington except on his collar and chest, and although Jefferson's face looked finished, his uncarved chin seemed to be propped on Washington's shoulder. Lincoln was only roughed out and barely recognizable.

Work continues on Jefferson. Throughout the carving, a work town of sheds, winch houses, walkways, and stairs crowned the four heads.

Since the beginning, a tram that was strung by cable from the base of the mountain to the top of Roosevelt's head had hoisted up tools in a large metal bucket, but water had to be hauled up the long winding staircase by hand in twenty-gallon cream cans at the rate of fifty or more a day. At last, during the 1935 season, a water supply was created, complete with reservoir, pumps, pipes, and modern facilities—a much-needed improvement.

An improvement that year for Lincoln Borglum was his promotion to chief pointer at $1.50 an hour. For several years he had worked on the mountain without pay, finally being hired as a pointer in 1934 at an hourly wage of 55¢. Now the twenty-three-year-old Lincoln was on his way up, not only as a pointer, but also as Mount Rushmore's official photographer. During the 1930s, the Eastman Kodak Company, which was experimenting with different kinds of film, provided Lincoln with elaborate cameras and color film to test on the spectacular scenery and dramatic working conditions at Rushmore. Lincoln carried a camera with him wherever he went and took candid shots of his father in a harness, drillers with their huge jackhammers, powder men loading their dynamite, and every other phase of the project, which now resembled a huge active quarry rather than an artistic undertaking. Lincoln's photos were widely distributed in magazines, newspapers, Rushmore brochures, history texts, travel books, and newsreels.

The year 1935 saw Senator Norbeck again trying to negotiate a federal loan. Borglum, who was incapable of staying out of the act if Rushmore was involved, was in Washington too, approaching congressmen and government officials with his own financial ideas, all of which were contrary to what Norbeck was trying to accomplish. Norbeck's displeasure can be imagined when he told Borglum, "I will not even start until you quit, for you will not harmonize your plans with the views of anyone else."

To add to Norbeck's difficulties, the "hard times" of the Depression made it almost impossible to raise federal funds for a distant mountain sculpture. "You cannot eat art," one congressman pointed out during the hearings. "Right now we should concentrate on the necessities of life."

Despite all the obstacles, not the least of which was Borglum's interference, Congress finally passed a bill in 1935 that granted $200,000 for Mount Rushmore. Temporarily, at least, the project was in solid financial shape, particularly because the matching-fund clause had been eliminated the year before and the $105,000 still left in that government account was turned over to the commission treasury in two annual payments.

A contest that the Hearst newspaper chain had run several months before had certainly helped boost passage of the bill. Asking for a 600-word history of the United States using essentially the same guidelines that Borglum had dictated to Calvin Coolidge back in 1927, Hearst offered $1000 for the prize-winning essay, implying that Borglum would sculpt the winning essay into the mountain. Although the entablature was never carved, and nothing more ever came of the winner's essay than came of Calvin Coolidge's literary efforts, over 800,000 essays were submitted. At long last, it seemed as if the American public was aroused by what Borglum was attempting to do on Mount Rushmore, and Congress, if nothing else, was sensitive to, and voted on, what concerned the American public.

Furthermore, part of President Roosevelt's New Deal policy was to sponsor federal projects around the country, and he had always been attracted to such out-of-the-ordinary ventures as Mount Rushmore. It didn't hurt, either, that his wife's uncle and his own distant cousin, Theodore Roosevelt, would one day gaze majestically down from a place of honor in the country's heartland.

· 11 ·

BY the beginning of the 1936 season, the relationship between Borglum and John Boland was so explosive that they were both anxious for the National Park Service to step into the situation. Borglum saw having a Park Service engineer in the now vacant superintendent's job as a way to bypass Boland and the commission, while Boland saw the Park Service as a buffer between Borglum and himself.

Because the superintendent of National Park Service memorials knew Borglum personally from having worked with him on an earlier sculpture in Washington, he was hesitant to involve the Park Service with Borglum and Rushmore in any way. But Boland, who was desperate, pressed his case, and finally, in July 1936, the Park Service appointed Julian Spotts as resident engineer at Mount Rushmore to keep Borglum in line, as well as to do everything possible to complete the memorial. Perhaps the dust storms and terrible heat of the Great Plains that Spotts drove through on his way to the Black Hills were an omen of what lay ahead at Rushmore.

As soon as he arrived, Spotts, a pleasant, soft-spoken man, began to make much-needed changes. He had the tram that hauled tools up to the top of the mountain strengthened, with a large wooden box added that

Borglum in the aerial tram that carried men as well as supplies to the top of Roosevelt's head.

would carry workers up to the heads so they wouldn't have to climb the 760-step stairway every morning, an improvement that Borglum had been urging for years. Spotts saw to it that the air compressor capability was increased so that twenty-two drills could be used at the same time. He had buildings repaired, the grounds cleaned up, and the physical plant put in good working order. But a federal administrator working with federal funds meant federal controls. And when Spotts began to impose Park Service regulations on Borglum's hiring practices, as well as ask for detailed timetables, statistics, estimates, and reports, Borglum balked. He had never worked that way and wasn't about to begin now.

So, eager as Borglum had been for a National Park Service engineer to step in, and efficient as Spotts had been in making improvements, which did, after all, free Borglum to concentrate his energies on the actual carving, within six weeks of Spotts's arrival, Borglum was in an uproar, complaining about the new regulations, about Spotts, and about the ridiculous Park Service rules. He argued with Spotts all summer over almost everything, and in one letter, Borglum stormed to his Washington friends about the "brainless jelly bean" he had to report to. Although their offices weren't more than a hundred yards apart, by the end of the summer, Borglum was communicating with Spotts by letter.

Despite the friction, which was nothing new for Borglum, work on the mountain continued at a good pace. Because funds were slow in arriving from Washington, the work season didn't begin until July 7, 1936, when Borglum put fifty men, including eleven drillers and eight carvers, to work in preparation for President Roosevelt's arrival on August 30. President Roosevelt, who had been persuaded to make a stopover in the Black Hills on his two-week tour of the nation's dust bowl, was eager to see the sculpture.

"Then Sunday I have got to have some place to go," he wrote, "and I was wondering whether . . . I could spend the day at Mount Rushmore. . . ." Not only was President Roosevelt welcome to visit Rushmore, but Borglum, always the opportunist, planned the Jefferson dedication for the occasion.

Although Borglum had arranged to have the ceremony start at noon when the light on Jefferson's face was best, the president and his party were delayed. Despite Borglum's angry threats to begin with or without the president, when the motorcade finally drove up at 2:30, Borglum was at his most charming.

Jefferson's face, like Washington's six years before, was draped with a

Borglum explaining the sculpture to President Franklin Roosevelt at the Jefferson dedication, August 30, 1936.

President Roosevelt speaks informally from his car at the Jefferson dedication.

huge American flag, with dynamite placed in strategic drill holes. Back on Doane Mountain, Borglum's daughter Mary Ellis waved an American flag, signaling her brother Lincoln up on top of Jefferson's head to detonate the dynamite. Three booming blasts raised an impressive cloud of gray dust as the flag was removed from Jefferson's face. At that moment a plane circled overhead and released small parachutes, each one bearing a flag and a chip of granite from the mountain. Although it was President Roosevelt's first experience with a Borglum dedication, it was nothing less than the other three thousand spectators had come to expect.

President Roosevelt wasn't prepared to speak, but when Borglum turned to him and said, "I want you, Mr. President, to dedicate this memorial as a shrine to democracy," he could hardly refuse.

The president, who had been paralyzed by polio fifteen years earlier, remained seated in his open car as he took the microphone. "I had had no conception until about ten minutes ago not only of its [Mount Rushmore's] magnitude, but of its permanent beauty and of its permanent importance." He added that the monument was an example of "cooperation with nature and not fighting with nature."

President Roosevelt had been caught up in the theory that Borglum had been expounding for years, that it was the artist's task to "free" the heads from the massive rock, that he must "try to find and release the faces of four great Americans within that granite mountain." Like other sculptors before him, Borglum believed that the sculpture he visualized was within the rock, waiting for his skill to liberate it.

President Roosevelt's Rushmore stopover, although brief, had left him as enthusiastic as the more than 200,000 tourists who visited the memorial that year. His next task wasn't such a pleasant one. He now continued on his much-publicized tour of the nation's heartland that had once been the fertile Great Plains and was now barren wasteland.

For centuries, buffalo had roamed over those thousands of square miles, feeding on the rich prairie grasses and in turn fertilizing the soil with their chips as well as their remains. Although there were many millions of buffalo, because they were constantly on the move, they never overgrazed or depleted the grass in any one area. Instead of fencing in the buffalo, the nomadic Plains Indians, who could pack up their entire village and be on the move in fifteen minutes, followed the buffalo wherever they roamed.

By the end of the nineteenth century, that way of life was finished forever. With the Indians confined to reservations, the homesteaders, farmers, and ranchers who staked out their claims on the Great Plains, plowed under the hardy natural grasses whose deep, extensive root systems conserved water and held the soil in place, planted crops with shallow roots, and fenced in their livestock. The continual planting of shallow-rooted crops such as wheat depleted the soil, and the domestic livestock soon overgrazed the land so that wind and water began to erode away the topsoil.

The years 1931 through 1938 saw one of the worst droughts in the country's history, with hot dry winds and almost no rain. The once rich soil became useless, as black clouds of dust blew up so thick that farmhouses were sometimes almost buried by sand dunes, people died of what was known as dust pneumonia, and countless herds of cattle perished or were slaughtered for lack of feed. In 1934, dust from the Great Plains blew as far east as the Atlantic Ocean, where it settled on ships at sea.

If the condition of the Great Plains farmers and ranchers was difficult, the plight of the Indians on the reservations was desperate. With no work available, and no hope for future work, with no buffalo to sustain them, without the right to hunt in the Black Hills as they once had when game was scarce, and dependent on the government for shelter, food, and clothing, the Indians lived in helpless, grinding poverty. Only federal work and economic programs provided any relief at all.

During one particularly severe winter during those Depression years, many of the Sioux on the Pine Ridge Reservation were literally starving to death. Gutzon Borglum, who could be, and often was, a warmly compassionate and generous person, heard about their situation and organized a committee to round up donations of livestock from all over the Black Hills. In an open letter to South Dakotans, he wrote, "The Indians are in a condition of want, unbelievable and unforgivable for us."

With Lincoln's help, Borglum collected a hundred head of cattle, some from his own ranch, and arranged to have them trucked to the reservation, along with food and clothing. Although the Sioux made both Borglums honorary members of their tribe in gratitude, perhaps a more lasting benefit would have been an offer of employment at Rushmore from Borglum, an offer that never came.

BECAUSE the men had to handle heavy equipment on the sheer rock face of the mountain at an elevation of over a mile, as well as work extensively with dynamite, virtually all jobs on Rushmore were dangerous. As Borglum himself said, "We needed and were developing in ourselves much courage, for much as we whistled over our job, we all imagined and were constantly aware of the proximity of . . . a very real graveyard all about us. Were we afraid? Certainly we were afraid, every mother's son of us, but I believed we enjoyed even that. [We] very soon became used to [our] situation between heaven and death and we lost thought of the hazard."

With those kinds of conditions, Borglum had every right to boast of his safety record, no deaths and no permanent injuries. Throughout all the years of carving, only two serious accidents occurred, both during the 1936 season.

The first accident was caused by the snapping of a sprocket chain on the new tramway, when the carriage, with five men aboard, was nearly to the top of the mountain. As the carriage hurtled down the fifteen hundred feet toward the bottom, all five men hit the emergency brake handle, breaking it instantly. Luckily, the quick-thinking foreman at the bottom shoved a two-by-four into the chute that fed out the cable, thus slamming the runaway carriage to a screeching halt. The only person hurt was a worker who panicked, jumped out of the speeding tram, and broke his arm and several ribs.

The second accident that summer occurred on a sunny, bright day at Rushmore while an electrical storm was raging in the nearby Keystone area. Lightning struck the Keystone generator, traveled three miles along the power line to Rushmore, knocked out the transformer at the base of the mountain, and ran up the power line to where a powder man was setting dynamite charges. The dynamite caps detonated, slamming the wooden tamping stick out of the powder man's hand, as well as blowing off a nearby driller's shoes and knocking a tourist unconscious on top of the mountain.

Perhaps the Sioux respect for their mountain spirits of thunder and lightning who danced among the granite peaks had some foundation in practicality. At least Borglum must have thought so. Although he had always insisted that all men leave the blasting area as soon as the dynamite was in place, he now suspended all dynamiting if there was an electrical storm anywhere in the vicinity. And it was shortly after the accident that the Mount Rushmore Memorial Commission prohibited tourists from going to the top of the mountain, a practice that had long been permitted.

Another close call that might have been even more disastrous occurred one day when both Borglum and Lincoln were gone from the site and the foreman of work took it upon himself to remove in one efficient blast an unsightly knob of granite behind Abraham Lincoln's head known as the "Three Monkeys." Instead of taking off the rock in layers as he had been ordered, the foreman had a line of eight-foot-deep holes drilled and loaded with dynamite.

Lincoln Borglum drove up just in time to hear the powder man yell, "Fire!" and see a chunk of rock fly straight out into the air for what seemed an eternity before crashing to the ground. Helpless, Lincoln watched the rock gather momentum as it thundered down the mountain demolishing everything in its path, including great pine trees that snapped like toothpicks. The juggernaut finally tumbled to a stop about a hundred feet in front of the blacksmith's shop at the base of the mountain, leaving Lincoln and the entire crew open-mouthed in horror.

Not fifteen minutes later, Borglum arrived and right away spotted the swath of cleared timber as wide as a ski trail all the way down the

mountainside. That foreman was one Rushmore employee who would never forget the impact of a Borglum tongue lashing.

At a time when there were no strict federal regulations regarding hardhats and safety shoes, the men usually wore cloth caps and everyday leather boots or sneakers. Despite the lack of federal laws, Borglum and his men evolved their own set of safety standards. An unwritten rule was that no one could unstrap the safety belt on his harness until he was on a level surface on top of the mountain. And Borglum made sure that the 300-foot-long cables on the winches that supported the men in their harnesses and swinging cages were carefully checked every day. Constructed of many feet of excess cable, sections that showed wear were cut out, usually the first five or six feet where the strain was the greatest.

Another safety precaution that Borglum insisted on was that the men had to be staggered on the mountain so that no one ever worked directly above anyone else in case a tool or piece of rock fell. Because the scaffolding was often more than one story, Borglum had the planks of the scaffolding floors constructed close enough together so that tools or stone chips couldn't fall through and injure anyone on the story below.

The granite itself presented a health problem. Breathing in the hard grainy granite dust was a recognized cause of the lung disease silicosis, and although masks and goggles were issued, the workers seldom bothered with them, particularly if the wind was blowing the dust away from their faces. As the official photographer of the sculpture-in-progress, Lincoln Borglum took many photographs that show the workers' faces and clothing so covered with granite dust that they appear to be working in a snowstorm.

With no treatment for silicosis known, the incurable disease sometimes doesn't manifest itself until years after exposure, causing such symptoms as shortness of breath, coughing, chest pain, and general weakness. There are no definite statistics, but it is known that two workmen have died from silicosis, several more have sought compensation for the condition, while others still suffer from it. Because many of the men were also hard-rock miners, they were exposed to rock dust in that capacity, too, making it difficult to pin down an exact cause-and-effect relationship. However, silicosis, which grates like sandpaper in the lungs, and which can lead to pneumonia, emphysema, chronic bronchitis, and heart disease, has been a problem over the years for a number of workers, adding a long-term risk to already dangerous conditions.

Undaunted by the accidents and the continuing friction with Spotts,

Workers, who wore soft hats and shoes for their dangerous work, often didn't bother with their masks.

Borglum accomplished more in the 1936 season than in any other period so far. Detailed work was done on the Washington and Jefferson heads, on Lincoln's brow, nose, and eyes, with excess rock taken off Washington's chest and from the areas under Jefferson's chin. And at last, after changing the studio model nine times, Borglum decided on the final location of Theodore Roosevelt, placing him between Jefferson and Lincoln.

Roosevelt, whose likeness had presented the greatest problem being accepted by the public, now presented Borglum with the greatest technical problems. There were so many cracks and crevices where Roosevelt's head was to be located, Borglum had to blast rock back a distance of 120 feet before he came to usable granite. Because there is a canyon only thirty feet behind Roosevelt's head, at one point Borglum was certain he would have to take Roosevelt out altogether and leave the space blank. But he persisted, and by the end of the 1936 season, after blasting off tons of rock, workmen were within five feet of the end of Roosevelt's nose. Actually, the fact that Roosevelt is recessed so far back may be appropriate for the man whom many felt should never have been included with the other three in the first place.

The National Park Service opened the 1937 season by dictating to Borglum exactly what it wanted him to accomplish during the coming year. It goes without saying how Borglum reacted to those suggestions, especially after the associate director of the Park Service publicly described him as "the very temperamental sculptor." Borglum quickly retorted that the sculpture was "no boy's job, nor road contractor's job and is not, must not and cannot be the victim of engineer's rule and compass."

With Borglum gone a good deal of the time, and Spotts and Lincoln Borglum, who was now foreman of work, in charge, the 1937 season went well despite its turbulent beginning. During that summer, most of the effort was concentrated on finishing Lincoln's face and roughing out Roosevelt, with almost nothing done on Washington or Jefferson.

Although he was often absent, Borglum's presence was always felt in the detailed instructions he forwarded. "I have marked Lincoln's eye," he wrote. "You can put two men in cages in each of the eyes. I would use Anderson on the one side and Bianco on the other, putting Bianco where the feldspar streaks run down, and Anderson on the outside. I would give Payne, with Bianco, a position on the nose and have them begin to take off stone by drilling in squares and breaking it off down to within six or seven inches of the finished surface. But do not try to cut the eyelid or eyeball. Make a round mass for each of these."

The lumps of rock on Lincoln's face, which anchor movable cages, were removed later.

Borglum, of course, was very much present on September 17, 1937, when the Lincoln head was dedicated in connection with the 150th anniversary of the adoption of the Constitution. Held only a year after the Jefferson dedication, it showed what kind of headway could be made with adequate funds and efficient management. This time five thousand people arrived at Doane Mountain to hear the speakers praise Lincoln and uphold the Constitution, although it was the final speaker, Gutzon Borglum, who, as usual, provided the drama.

After a roll call of Mount Rushmore supporters who had died, including Calvin Coolidge, Charles E. Rushmore, Joseph S. Cullinan, former chairman of the Mount Rushmore National Memorial Commission, and Senator Peter Norbeck, who had died of cancer the year before, Borglum proclaimed, "They are with the gods! We will keep their faith! We will carry on!" After a brief silence, a trooper, who was suspended to the side of Washington's head a quarter of a mile away, played taps, the clear bugle notes carrying out over the hushed crowd.

Borglum continued, with such sweeping praise of the sculpture as "an immortal work of fine art . . . a masterpiece of great sculpture . . . great pioneer and cultural adventure . . . an accomplishment without parallel in this or the old world." In conclusion, he turned to his daughter: "Mary Ellis, will you call to your brother to fire the blast and unveil the portrait of Abraham Lincoln?" At the signal, Lincoln Borglum detonated the dynamite, and the American flag that covered the Lincoln head was pulled aside. A vocal solo of "Weeping Water" and "The Star-Spangled Banner" led by the Homestake Band and the Band of the 4th Cavalry, concluded the ceremony.

In spite of increasing interest in Rushmore around the country, and in spite of the ever-growing number of tourists, more than 265,000 in 1937, the 1938 season couldn't have gotten off to a worse start. Borglum, who claimed that he hadn't been paid for his work the year before, refused even to show up at the mountain, although he did send Lincoln to the Black Hills to begin work on May 9. While Lincoln started up operations, Borglum remained in Washington to lobby Congress for more federal funds. Almost more important to him than the money was his determination to get the sculpture out of the hands of the commission, not to mention the National Park Service, which he was now calling "a Frankenstein."

By 1938, Borglum's relationship with the Park Service and the commission, especially his old nemesis, John Boland, had become unworkable. Borglum wrote angry letters to everyone even remotely connected with the project, from President Roosevelt on down, about how his working conditions had become unbearable under the "destructive influence" of both the commission and the Park Service. Borglum was anxious to replace the old commission with a new, friendly commission that he could hand-pick, and who would rubber-stamp everything he asked for. Above all, he wanted to be rid of John Boland.

With the help of Washington friends, many of whom were legislators familiar with his impressive head of Lincoln in the Capitol rotunda, Borglum lobbied, testified, and buttonholed anyone who would listen to him, and in June 1938, he won everything he had fought for. Congress created a new twelve-person commission, relieving the old commission and the Park Service of all responsibility. Congress also set aside twelve hundred acres to be known as the Mount Rushmore Memorial Reservation. To top off the victory, Congress appropriated $300,000 for continuing work on the project, all funding to come directly through the Treasury Department.

John Boland, who had devoted nine years of his life to Mount Rushmore on the Memorial Commission, and who had become as dedicated to the completion of the project as Borglum, albeit on different terms, had wisely and frugally kept the project financially alive through its early, most difficult years. Now he realized that he and Borglum could no longer work together, and he knew that while he, as a businessman, was replaceable, Borglum, as the sculptor, was not. It was time for him to resign, a bitter moment. It wasn't until 1941, when Boland was unanimously elected president of the Mount Rushmore National Memorial Society, that he again became a part of the Rushmore picture.

In many ways, the Park Service was relieved to be done with Mount Rushmore, a project that had always run counter to its conservationist policies, and perhaps being done with Borglum was a relief as well. Over the years, the Service had amassed a thick file labeled "Mount Rushmore Borglum Controversy." Now that file could be closed.

CHAPTER
· 13 ·

F O R Gutzon Borglum, the 1938 season was the best of times. Now that all funds were coming through the Treasury Department and he was working with a commission that President Roosevelt had appointed from his suggestions, he was free to do as he pleased.

From the beginning, Borglum had wanted to work straight through the year, and now he did just that, missing only three weeks during the winter of 1938–39 because of bad weather. To keep the men warm, he covered the scaffolding with heavy canvas tarpaulins and burned wood in fifty-five-gallon drums, making sure that the drums were set far enough back on the scaffolding so that the heat wouldn't shatter the icy granite. Prestone in the air hoses kept the air from freezing, although work had to stop temporarily when the temperature dropped to less than twenty degrees below zero.

Difficult conditions or not, it suited the men fine to be employed full-time, and the extended season didn't hurt Borglum financially either. With the twenty-five percent commission he earned on all monies spent on the project, in 1938 he earned $16,013, an impressive sum during the Depression, considering that the congressmen to whom he was constantly appealing for funds earned $10,000.

What excited Borglum even more than working through the winter that banner year of 1938 was being able to start on what was closest to his heart, the Hall of Records. Up until now, the original commission and the National Park Service had confined Borglum to concentrating on the four heads. But Borglum believed that the Hall of Records, which he had designed in careful detail, was every bit as important as the sculpture.

The Hall of Records was to be a cave, one hundred feet deep by eighty feet wide by thirty-two feet high. It would be excavated out of the wall of the canyon behind the four heads, the same canyon that had presented such a problem in locating the Roosevelt head. In Borglum's words, it

With all four pointing machines still in use, canvas tarpaulins on the Roosevelt scaffolding protect workers from the cold during the winter of 1938–39.

Gutzon Borglum's son, Lincoln, appointed superintendent in 1938 to oversee all aspects of the sculpture, here inspects the air compressor hoses.

OPPOSITE: Work begins on the Hall of Records in the canyon behind the heads.

would hold "the records of our republic, its successful creation; the record of its western movement to the Pacific; its presidents; how the memorial was built; and frankly why."

Included in the Hall would be permanent scrolls describing American inventions and achievements in science, art, literature, medicine, and government, as well as twenty-five statues of important Americans from Benjamin Franklin through President Franklin D. Roosevelt, not to mention Susan B. Anthony, whom Borglum included to appease the women who had fought to have her likeness on the mountain itself. "Her friends will be happy," he declared.

A long granite stairway with steps fifteen feet wide would start at Borglum's studio on Doane Mountain, rise gradually up to the canyon north of Lincoln's head, and from there continue up to the entrance of the great Hall of Records. Borglum also included in the plans the historical inscription he had wanted on the mountain ever since he had begun the carving, but which he had been forced to abandon for lack of space.

The enormity of the plans stunned everyone who saw them, the excavation of the mountain, the 800-foot long stairway, the sculpting of the statues, the gathering together of records and artifacts, the sinking of a time capsule. But Borglum was determined. This was for eternity, he announced, so that thousands of years from now when people viewed those four heads, they would know who the granite faces represented and what had been accomplished in the greatest civilization the world had ever known. Because he insisted that the project was for posterity and not for personal glory, he refused to have his name inscribed anywhere on the mountain, a modest decision for one whom many considered to be a supreme egotist.

Now an aging seventy-one, Borglum appointed his son Lincoln to be superintendent in 1938, at $4800 a year. Lincoln, who had worked at almost every position on the mountain, took over many of the administrative duties, as well as supervision of the almost daily work on Roosevelt's face and the finishing on Washington's neck and coat lapel. But on February 24, 1939, while his father was in Washington applying for more money, funds ran out and Lincoln had to stop all work.

Meanwhile, in Washington, Borglum was being pinned down by congressional committees increasingly impatient with what had become Rushmore's annual appeal for money. How much longer will the carving take? Will this amount complete the sculpture? What if you need more funds? Despite certain legislators' unhappiness with all the delays, as

well as with Borglum's elaborate plans for the Hall of Records, Congress voted to allow Borglum to use the entire $250,000 left in the Treasury Department account, provided that he finish the sculpture by June 1940.

Even though it was clear that practically no one was enthusiastic about the Hall of Records, during the next months Borglum put all his energies, and $16,000 of federal money, into blasting a tunnel into the mountain, seventy-five feet deep, fourteen feet high, and twenty feet wide. But by July 1939, even Borglum's friendly, hand-picked commission, which he called "my commission," was beginning to question the wisdom of continuing work on the Hall. After all, although Borglum was now giving his age as sixty-eight, it was common knowledge that he was seventy-two and in failing health. And he was the only person who could supervise the artistic finishing of the faces.

Under pressure, Borglum reluctantly turned his attention back to the heads, personally taking charge of work on Roosevelt and the final finishing on Washington and Jefferson. At least he now had enough funds to hire skilled carvers, a lack he had been bemoaning for years. But to his surprise, with the exception of Luigi Del Bianco, few of the carvers worked out. By the time a carver was highly skilled, he had usually reached middle age, and the prospect of working in a harness or a swinging cage on the windy mountain held so little appeal that if any of them even started, they soon quit. Even Del Bianco always worked from a cage, refusing from the start ever to be lowered over the mountain in a harness.

"There are no mountain granite sculptors in America," Borglum admitted, perhaps appreciating for the first time how skilled his hard-rock miners and out-of-work ranchers and loggers had become in their years of drilling, blasting, carving, and finishing.

And they had learned to work quickly as well as efficiently. On July 2, 1939, less than two years after the Lincoln dedication, the Roosevelt head was dedicated, a celebration that was combined with South Dakota's fiftieth anniversary of statehood. This time, Borglum, who had masterminded five similar ceremonies over the years, elected to hold the dedication at night. Theodore Roosevelt, who had spent a good deal of time in South Dakota and written widely about his western experiences, was popular with South Dakotans, and twelve thousand people arrived for the spectacular.

A bright moon was the only source of light as the crowd gazed up at the faces, Roosevelt's veiled by the usual American flag. Without warning, brilliant rockets and aerial bombs exploded, lighting up the whole

An unfinished Roosevelt, whose carved eyeglasses create an optical illusion, is dedicated, July 2, 1939.

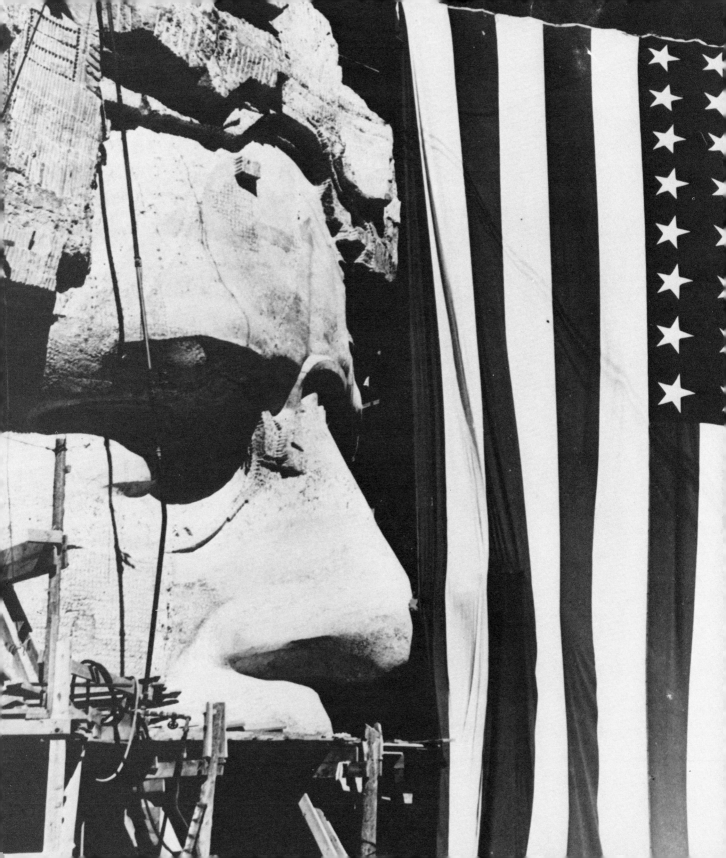

mountain. As soon as the fireworks faded, Borglum gave the signal for powerful searchlights to shine on the heads. With Sioux Indians in full native dress and movie celebrities making their dramatic appearance, no one present could doubt that Borglum had again topped his own past efforts.

Appearances to the contrary, the dedication had come at a time of great personal stress for Borglum. Only the day before, President Franklin Roosevelt had announced that because Mount Rushmore would be supervised by the National Park Service in the Department of the Interior after it was completed, he wanted the sculpture returned to the National Park Service.

Although Borglum's howl of protest could probably be heard all the way to Washington, on the other side of the coin, the Park Service and the Department of the Interior weren't all that thrilled either. Following the transfer, Secretary of the Interior Ickes wrote to President Roosevelt, "When I have anything official to do in connection with Mr. Gutzon Borglum's enterprise at Mount Rushmore I always feel like equipping myself as a man does when he fusses with a beehive."

Knowing that the Park Service would probably kill his dream of completing his beloved Hall of Records, as well as put an end to the financially inefficient winter work season, Borglum complained that the transfer "put me right back where I was, at the mercy of unsympathetic men who have no idea of how life can be given to blocks of granite."

Clearly, in Borglum's mind, no one understood how important the Hall of Records, the inscription, and the grand stairway were. Aging he may have been, but Borglum was as articulate as ever. "You might as well drop a letter into the world's postal service without an address or signature, as to send that carved mountain into history without identification."

But Borglum's objections were to no avail, and he must have known as well as anyone that if he wanted continued financial support from the government, he had to go along with the president's decision. Still, the change of power meant just what he feared. The National Park Service declared that the Hall of Records, the inscription, and the stairway could all be built by qualified Park Service engineers following Borglum's plans, but the final finishing of the heads required the presence of the master. So Borglum had to abandon his Hall of Records, which was never worked on again, its deep cave becoming instead a snug haven for mountain goats during the Black Hills winters.

Another frustration for Borglum in 1939 was that 300,000 tourists were now visiting Rushmore each year, and it must have seemed that they were all crowding into his studio at once, to watch him work, examine his studio model, and buy postcards and souvenirs. What Borglum needed were new working quarters, and that summer construction was begun at a site 250 feet northeast of his log studio which was eventually turned into a visitors' center.

But like everything else involving Borglum, the move wasn't made without difficulty. The Park Service sent Borglum blueprints for the studio, but after looking them over, Borglum asked a friend to draw up new plans and then threw the Park Service blueprints in the wastebasket.

Both 1939 and 1940 were difficult for Borglum, who was constantly frustrated by Park Service demands and controls. With war raging in Europe, even President Roosevelt, who had more serious matters on his mind, sounded weary when he wrote to the Speaker of the House in 1939, "I should like to see the work at Mount Rushmore finally wound up."

Although the funds, including the final $86,000 that Congress appropriated in 1940 for the 1941 season, were still being funneled through the Treasury Department, it was the Park Service which was again pulling the strings, leaving Borglum's friendly commission still functioning, but basically powerless. By now Borglum was in increasingly bad health, and although Lincoln was taking more and more responsibility, it was still his father who had to direct the refining and finishing work on all four faces, a task that consumed almost the entire 1940 season.

The following year, 1941, while in Chicago with his wife for a radio appearance, Borglum underwent routine surgery. Although he seemed to be recovering, he took an unexpected turn for the worse, and his children rushed to Chicago to be with him. On March 6, 1941, after a life of tumult and controversy, Gutzon Borglum died.

In many ways, Borglum, a product of the early western frontier, was a complex man, just as the Black Hills where he labored for the last fourteen years of his life was a complex environment, both subject to sudden violent storms and bright sunlight, both larger than life, enduring, as well as occasionally crass and commercial. But no matter what Borglum's faults were, nor what criticism was leveled against him about his temperament, his artistic ability, or his strong-arm methods of getting what he wanted, the fact that he saw his vision become a reality by accomplishing what he set out to do against great odds can never be denied him.

CHAPTER
· 14 ·

IMMEDIATELY after Borglum's death, the commission asked

IMMEDIATELY after Borglum's death, the commission asked Lincoln to continue on as superintendent at Mount Rushmore to finish up what he could with the remaining funds "in accordance with the known plans, models and specifications of the late Gutzon Borglum." A month later, the commission appointed Lincoln Sculptor of the project, the title his father had held for so many years.

Throughout that summer of 1941, Lincoln did everything he could to leave the memorial in the best possible condition. After having worked in almost every capacity on the mountain, Lincoln knew exactly what needed to be done, and how to do it. With the finishing work almost completed by his father, that summer Lincoln worked on the Roosevelt face, cleaned up Washington's heavy jaw, blocked out Jefferson's collar, and finished up Lincoln's beard.

October 31, 1941, was the last day of drilling, almost fourteen years to the day from when drilling had first begun. It was a sad occasion as Lincoln Borglum supervised the removal of stone from the top of Jefferson's head, and took away ledges where the scaffolding had been anchored. The next few weeks were spent generally cleaning up, taking

The 1941 season sees final finishing work done on all four heads.

down the tramway, and dismantling everything from the top of the heads to bring it down the mountain for storage.

Lincoln's final report in November stated, "I do not think any more should be done on figures of the Memorial. It looks very well as it is and I think it is more effective this way, than if carried down as shown on the models." He added, "I believe that it is very essential that the Hall of Records and the stairway leading to it, be completed."

But the National Park Service, which took over control of Mount Rushmore in September 1941, did not have, nor has ever had, any interest in completing the Hall of Records, or in building the grand stairway which was so important to both Borglums. In 1942 the Director of the Park Service commented about these projects, "Definitely out as far as we are concerned."

With the entry of the United States into World War II in December 1941, all suggestions for further work on Rushmore, including the removal of the tons of rock beneath the heads left over from the blasting, were tabled, never to be considered seriously again. As the Memorial exists now, the 300-foot-deep pile of shattered rock, interspersed with new ponderosa pine growth, makes an appropriately dramatic setting for the acre-and-a-half surface of mountain covered by the four heads.

During the years of carving, the government funneled a total of $836,000 into the project, with another $153,992.32 coming from fundraising events and from corporations and individuals, the largest contributor being Gutzon Borglum himself. Although no more money was ever spent on the actual carvings, over the years the Park Service has greatly improved the 1278-acre Memorial grounds which, along with Harney National Forest, are now a part of the Black Hills National Forest. Parking lots, an amphitheater, a visitor center, a concession building, a viewing terrace, walks and trails, night lighting, as well as a museum in what was once Borglum's studio, have all been part of Rushmore's development.

The National Park Service annually inspects the heads, lowering a worker down in a harness by Borglum's old sturdy winch-and-cable apparatus to seal any cracks with Borglum's formula of granite dust, white lead, and linseed oil, to prevent moisture from collecting that might freeze and split the granite. Otherwise, the Park Service never touches or cleans the heads. Their scrubbed-white appearance is a result of the polishing and bleaching effects of the weather and the depth to which Borglum had to blast into the rock.

The National Park Service inspects the heads annually. The wide bands on Lincoln's face are lighter-colored and coarser-textured rock, not cracks.

Although the sculpture has been criticized over the years for defacing the innate beauty of the mountain itself, and criticized artistically for its romantic naturalism and colossal size, the reaction of the two million visitors a year who view it cannot be dismissed. Upon first seeing the sculpture, they are often silent, speaking in hushed tones as if they were indeed at a shrine. Certainly the scale studio model from which the heads were directly carved would not be considered great art under any circumstances, so it must be the size of the sculpture that inspires such awe . . . or its setting . . . or a stirring of patriotism . . . or a realization of what an engineering feat the heads represent . . . or perhaps it is a combination of all these, a somehow throat-catching symbol of this country, just as Borglum had planned it to be, embodying in its conception, size, and spirit what the American dream is all about.

For the Sioux Indians, the four heads represent something entirely different. After all, Mount Rushmore and the Black Hills were, and are, their sacred land, at the center of their universe, and realizing that the sculpture has become a national symbol, they have used the mountain to make their own statement. Led by leaders of AIM, the American Indian Movement, in 1972 and 1973, Sioux Indians from the Pine Ridge Reservation camped all summer behind Mount Rushmore, occasionally demonstrating on top of the heads for the return of their rightful land, Paha Sapa, awarded to them by the 1868 Fort Laramie Treaty. They were also demonstrating for the return of 200,000 acres at Pine Ridge that were used as a bombing test site during World War II.

Another sympathetic group demonstrated at Rushmore in 1973, this time in support of the Indians who were occupying the nearby town of Wounded Knee. Even today, Indians periodically occupy some part or another of the Black Hills to stake out their claim for the return of their land.

In 1923 the Sioux filed a petition with the United States Court of Claims accusing the government of taking the Black Hills without fair payment, in violation of the Fifth Amendment to the Constitution. "No person shall be . . . deprived of life, liberty, or property, without due process of law; nor shall private property be taken for public use, without just compensation."

Since then, the case has been in and out of the courts until 1980 when the Supreme Court handed down a landmark decision to award $17.5 million to the Sioux, plus five percent interest. This amount represents the financial worth of the Black Hills in 1877 when the United

Pine trees flourish in the tons of shattered rock blasted off the mountain.

States government illegally acquired the land. It was the first occasion in United States history that any branch of the government not only admitted that Indian land was unconstitutionally taken, but also awarded payment for the land, with interest. Nevertheless, the decision has left many Sioux dissatisfied. Rather than the money, they want their land returned, their sacred Paha Sapa.

Most of those concerned Sioux still live on the Pine Ridge Reservation, the second largest Indian reservation in the nation, with some 18,400 people scattered over forty-five hundred square miles. According to statistics of the Bureau of Indian Affairs, only fifteen percent of the entire Pine Ridge work force between the ages of sixteen and sixty-five were employed in 1983, and of those employed, twelve percent earned less than the minimum wage. Tribal leaders claim a ninety percent unemployment rate. And all this just a little more than a century after the Sioux were considered to be the most powerful Indian tribe in America.

Only thirty miles from Pine Ridge, the Black Hills and Mount Rushmore have become a national recreational and vacation mecca. The gold rush days of the 1870s and 1880s are long since gone, but the smell of the pine, the rushing streams, the grassy meadows, steep canyons, the stillness of vast limestone caves, the jagged mountain peaks, and of course, those four familiar granite faces have attracted many more people than the promise of gold ever did.

Certainly, Mount Rushmore and the Black Hills, close to the geographical center of the United States, have touched many people in many ways. To the Sioux, the Black Hills have been unique and special, a place of spirits. To Gutzon Borglum, Mount Rushmore meant an opportunity to express what his country meant to him and to immortalize that vision to the world. To the millions of visitors every year, to view Mount Rushmore is a singular experience, which allows each person to interpret individually the significance of this ancient granite mountain.

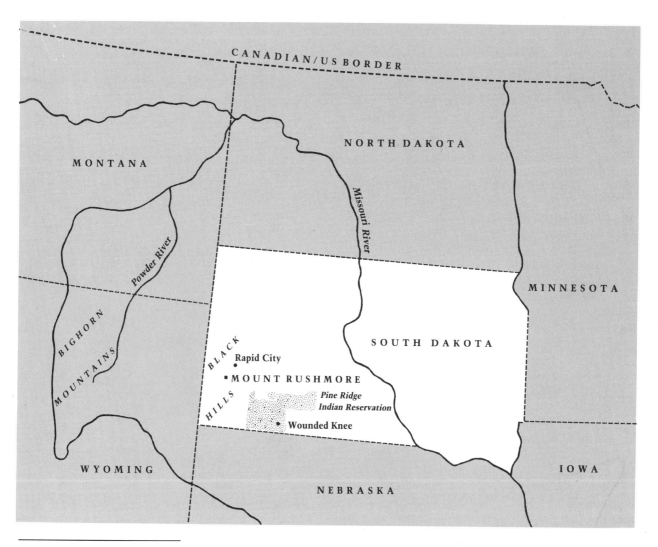

Ambrose, Stephen E. *Crazy Horse and Custer.* Garden City, N.Y.: Doubleday & Co., Inc., 1975.

American Heritage. *Indians of the Plains.* Narrative by Eugene Rachlis. New York: American Heritage Publishing Co., Inc., 1960.

Anderson, Adrienne B. "Archeological Assessment." Lincoln, Neb.: Mount Rushmore National Memorial, National Park Service, 1974.

Athearn, Robert G. *Age of Steel.* Vol. 10 of *The American Heritage New Illustrated History of the United States.* New York: Dell Publishing Co., Inc., 1963.

———. *The Frontier.* Vol. 6 of *The American Heritage New Illustrated History of the United States.* New York: Dell Publishing Co., Inc., 1963.

———. *Winning the West.* Vol. 9 of *The American Heritage New Illustrated History of the United States.* New York: Dell Publishing Co., Inc., 1963.

Borglum, Gutzon. "Aesthetic Activities in America: An Answer to His Critics." *The Craftsman* 15, no. 3 (December 1908): 301ff.

———. "Engineering Problems to Be Met in Mountain Sculpture." *The Black Hills Engineer* 18, no. 4 (November 1930): 308ff.

———. "Individuality, Sincerity and Reverence in American Art." *The Craftsman* 15, no. 1 (October 1908): 3ff.

———. "The Political Importance and the Art Character of the National Memorial at Mount Rushmore." *The Black Hills Engineer* 18, no. 4 (November 1930): 285ff.

———. "What Is Beauty in Sculpture?" *The Black Hills Engineer* 18, no. 4 (November 1930): 304ff.

Borglum, Lincoln. *My Father's Mountain.* Rapid City, S.D.: Fenwinn Press, 1965.

Borglum, Lincoln, with DenDooven, Gweneth Reed. *Mount Rushmore: Heritage of America.* Las Vegas: KC Publications, 1977.

Brown, Dee. *Bury My Heart at Wounded Knee.* New York: Holt, Rinehart & Winston, 1970.

———. *The Westerners.* New York: Holt, Rinehart & Winston, 1974.

Capps, Benjamin. *The Old West.* New York: Time-Life Books, Inc., 1975.

Casey, Robert J., and Borglum, Mary. *Give the Man Room.* New York: The Bobbs-Merrill Co., Inc., 1952.

Coburn, Mark D. "The Great Stone Faces." *Natural History* 86, no. 1 (January 1977): 60ff.

Cohen, Stan. *Borglum's Mountain.* Missoula, Mont.: Pictorial Histories Publishing Company, 1983.

Connolly, Joseph P. "The Geology of Mount Rushmore and Vicinity." *The Black Hills Engineer* 18, no. 4 (November 1930): 355ff.

Dary, David A. *The Buffalo Book.* Chicago: The Swallow Press, Inc., 1974.

Dean, Robert J. *Living Granite.* New York: The Viking Press, 1949.

Erdoes, Richard. *The Sun Dance People.* New York: Alfred A. Knopf, Inc., 1972.

Fichter, George S. *How the Plains Indians Lived.* New York: David McKay Co., 1980.

Fishbein's Illustrated Medical and Health Encyclopedia, vol. 20. Westport, Conn.: H. S. Stuttman Inc., Publishers, 1981.

Fite, Gilbert C. "Gutzon Borglum, Mercurial Master." *Montana Magazine of Western History* 25, no. 2 (Spring 1975): 2ff.

———. *Mount Rushmore.* Norman, Okla.: University of Oklahoma Press, 1952.

Froiland, Sven G. *Natural History of the Black Hills.* Sioux Falls, S.D.: The Center for Western Studies, 1978.

Goodson, Rose Mary. *The Rushmore Story.* Piedmont, S.D.: Rose Mary Goodson, 1979.

Hofsinde, Robert. *The Indian and the Buffalo.* New York: William Morrow Co., 1961.

Kappler, Charles J., ed. and comp. *Indian Treaties, 1778–1883.* New York: Interland Publishing, Inc., 1972.

Lauber, Patricia. *Dust Bowl.* New York: Coward-McCann, Inc., 1958.

Lincoln, Francis Church. "Engineering Practices at the Mount Rushmore National Memorial." *The Black Hills Engineer* 18, no. 4 (November 1930): 349ff.

Marvin, George. "Gutzon Borglum." *The World's Work* (June 1914): 198ff.

Matthiessen, Peter. *In the Spirit of Crazy Horse.* New York: The Viking Press, 1980.

McCullough, David. *Mornings on Horseback.* New York: Simon & Schuster, 1981.

Mount Rushmore National Memorial Commission. Brochures and pamphlets. Washington, D.C.: United States Department of the Interior, National Park Service, 1941.

Mount Rushmore National Memorial Files. Keystone, S.D.: National Park Service.

O'Harra, Cleophas C. "The Black Hills, Birthplace of America." *The Black Hills Engineer* 18, no. 4 (November 1930): 301ff.

_____. "Custer's Black Hills Expedition of 1874." *The Black Hills Engineer* 18, no. 4 (November 1930): 221ff.

The Oxford Companion to Art. Edited by Harold Osborne. Oxford: The Clarendon Press, 1970.

Parker, Watson, and Lambert, Hugh K. *Black Hills Ghost Towns.* Chicago: Sage Books, The Swallow Press, Inc., 1974.

Petsch, Bruno C., and McGregor, Duncan J. *South Dakota's Rock History.* Rapid City, S.D.: Educational Series 3 of the Devereaux Library, South Dakota School of Mines and Technology.

Price, Willadene. *Gutzon Borglum.* Copyright Willadene Price, 1961.

Rapid City Journal. Articles. Rapid City, S.D., 1970–1974.

Rezatto, Helen. *Tales of the Black Hills.* Aberdeen, S.D.: North Plains Press, 1983.

Robinson, Doane. "Inception and Development of the Rushmore Idea." *The Black Hills Engineer* 18, no. 4 (November 1930): 334ff.

Shuttlesworth, Dorothy. *The Story of Rocks.* Garden City, N.Y.: Doubleday & Co., Inc., 1956.

Sneve, Virginia Driving Hawk. *Dakota's Heritage.* Sioux Falls, S.D.: Brevet Press, 1973.

South Dakota, A Guide to the State. Revised by M. L. Reese. American Guide Series. New York: Hastings House, 1952.

United States Department of the Interior. Files and folders. Washington, D.C.: National Park Service.

United States National Archives. Records, correspondence, photographs. Washington, D.C.: National Park Service.

"United States, Petitioner, v. Sioux Nation of Indians et al." (Argued March 24, 1980; decided June 30, 1980). In *United States Supreme Court Reports* 65, nos. 79–639 (October Term, 1979): 844ff. Rochester, N.Y.: The Lawyers Co-Operative Publishing Co., 1981.

Upton, Robert F. "Mount Rushmore Speaks." In *Mount Rushmore: Shrine of Democracy.* Washington, D.C.: United States Department of the Interior, National Park Service, 1955.

Watkins, T. H. "The Terrible-Tempered Mr. Ickes." *Audubon* 86, no. 2 (March 1984): 94ff.

Wellman, Paul I. *Indian Wars and Warriors West.* Boston: Houghton Mifflin Co., 1959.

Zeitner, June Culp, and Borglum, Lincoln. *Borglum's Unfinished Dream, Mount Rushmore.* Aberdeen, S.D.: North Plains Press, 1976.

· Index ·

Numbers in italic refer to photographs.

Devereaux Library, South Dakota School of Mines and Technology: pp. 57, 77.

Library of Congress: pp. 33, 38 (bottom), 39 (top).

Modern Physical Geography by A. N. Strahler. (New York: John Wiley & Sons Inc., 1978.): p. 45. Reprinted with permission.

Mount Rushmore by Gilbert C. Fite. (Norman, Okla.: University of Oklahoma Press, 1952.): pp. 67, 103. Reprinted with permission.

Museum of Fine Arts, Boston: pp. 38 (top).

National Park Service, Department of the Interior: pp. 2, 3, 4, 12, 15, 16, 17, 40, 49, 52, 55, 56, 58, 59, 61, 63, 65, 66, 71, 73, 79, 83, 85, 89, 91, 92, 96, 99, 105, 107, 111, 112, 115, 126, 127.

Newark Public Library: p. 28.

South Dakota State Historical Society: pp. 29, 30.

South Dakota Tourism Photo: p. 23.

The Rushmore–Borglum Story, Keystone, South Dakota: p. 20.

Theodore Roosevelt Collection, Harvard College Library: p. 39 (bottom).

Diagram on p. 46 by Philip St. George.

921   St. George, Judith
BO

The Mount Rushmore
story

DATE		
OCT. 1 8 1991	NOV 2 2 2000	
DEC 2 1991		
MAR 4 1994	Feb 15 2002	
SEP. 2 6 1994	JUL 0 9 2002	
OCT 2 6 1994	JAN 9 2003	
JAN 2 0 1995	FEB 1 1 2003	
FEB 6 1995	FEB 2 6 2003	
APR 2 8 1995	MAR 1 7 2003	
JUL 2 1 1995	JUL 1 5 2005	
AUG 2 2 1996	AUG 2012	
MAR 3 0 1998	AUG 1 4 2012	
APR 3 0 1998	AUG 2 9 2012	
JUN 5 1998	APR 3 0 2015	
FEB 1 0 2000		